PRAISE FOR
GRIEVING THE WRITE WAY

"Healing from a loss is the hardest work one will ever have to do. To do it well, we need help to walk head on into the grief each day. That's where Gary's book *Grieving the Write Way* comes in. This is such a tremendous tool for the challenge of moving forward by journaling and getting honest with your emotions and memories as you process and progress on your journey toward healing. Thank you, Gary Roe!"

- Rosemary Rhodes, fellow griever and
seasoned traveler on the grief journey

"I have always loved journaling and writing. That's why Gary Roe's *Grieving the Write Way Journal and Workbook* is the perfect fit for me. I love the journaling prompts and the many creative ways included in the book, like poetry, letters, and stories designed to help in processing my emotions and sorting out my thoughts. When I feel alone and grief overwhelms me, this workbook is the perfect companion to steady my walk and help me express my mind, heart, and soul."

- Hadassah Treu, Christian Author,
Blogger and Speaker

"I read *Grieving the Write Way* 20 months after the loss of my wife of 50 years. Grief is a lonely and traumatic experience that rears its ugly head without warning at the most unexpected times. This book, with stories and quotes from other grief-stricken individuals, tells you that you are not alone on this journey, and gives you hope that somehow you will survive this ordeal, and that there will be a future. In his caring, thoughtful, and affable way, Gary draws you in to the writing exercises in the journal portions of the book. Writing about my grief is something I had never considered, but it is so helpful and thought provoking to actually get your feelings down on paper. I know this book will be a constant companion and resource for me as I, over time, reengage in the writing exercises and measure my progress."

- Dennis Baer, bereaved spouse and
survivor of multiple close losses

"*Grieving the Write Way* was mesmerizing to me. I found myself absorbed in the readings, exercises, and activities. This workbook is an invaluable tool in guiding the grieving heart to finding the pathway to comfort and healing."

- Brian Kenney, Pastor and fellow griever

"Once again, Gary Roe has been able to reach into those difficult places in the journey of grief and offer real-life help and encouragement. With genuine compassion and wisdom drawn from his own journeys through grief, Gary prompts the reader to look at the emotions and realities of grief and process them with healthy, honest, and productive methods and suggestions. Written in short topical chapters, this is a tool that you must have as you navigate the hard season of grief."

- Lynette McCombs, fellow griever

"After losing my only child 33 months ago, I learned so much from *Grieving the Write Way*. This book is a definite must-have for any person that is grieving the death of a loved one. Thank you once for your commitment to help all the grieving hearts out there."

- Elrina Vinter, bereaved mom,
South Africa

"Grieving is necessary to help us assimilate ourselves to our new life after a devastating loss. *Grieving the Write Way* is a grief book that can slow you down and help you work through your thoughts and feelings. I found reading and journaling with the direction of author Gary Roe to be very cathartic. I like going back to see what I wrote."

- Jane Machut, fellow griever, Brookfield, Wisconsin

"*Grieving the Write Way* helps the reader to think and write about the many different feelings that the grieving person experiences. The book/journal format supports one in navigating the grief journey by assisting in processing those difficult emotions to help heal after loss."

- Susan, bereaved spouse

"I find it hard to process grief, as when I'm in the thick of it, the waves of grief seem to drown everything out. In *Grieving the Write Way*, I especially found the writing prompts Gary provides to be an incredibly helpful means of beginning to process grief when I didn't know how to articulate it. I highly recommend for anyone who feels like they need help to process any kind of grief."

- Stephanie Stevenson, fellow griever and MK (Missionary Kids) Advisor, WEC Canada

"If you're grieving this is a must have. Commentary and writing exercises to help you describe your feelings. Great to look back on when you're further down your grief journey so you can look back and see how far you've come and realize that you CAN do this. Would be awesome for grief groups or as a personal resource."

- Dawn Combs, Angel Mom since 2014

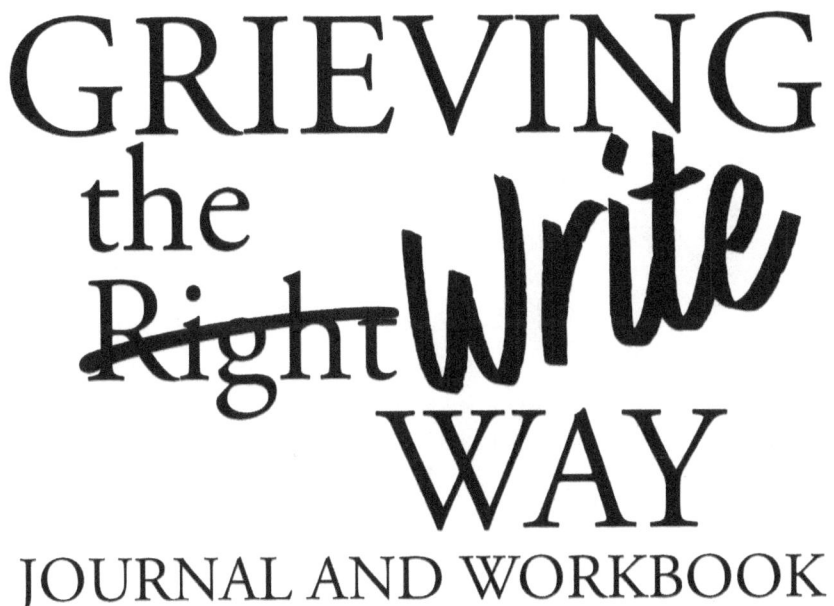

JOURNAL AND WORKBOOK

GARY ROE

Grieving the Write Way Journal and Workbook
Copyright © 2021 by Gary Roe All rights reserved.
First Edition:

Print ISBN: 978-1-950382-47-7
Print (KDP) ISBN: 978-1-950382-46-0
eBook ISBN: 978-1-950382-48-4

Cover and Formatting: Streetlight Graphics

Published by: Healing Resources Publishing

All Bible references are from THE HOLY BIBLE, NEW INTERNATIONAL VERSION®, NIV® Copyright © 1973, 1978, 1984, 2011 by Biblica, Inc.® Used by permission. All rights reserved worldwide.

The author is not engaged in rendering medical or psychological services, and this book is not intended as a guide to diagnose or treat medical or psychological problems. If you require medical, psychological, or other expert assistance, please seek the services of your own physician or mental health professional.

No part of this book may be reproduced, scanned, or distributed in any printed or electronic form without permission. Please do not participate in or encourage piracy of copyrighted materials in violation of the author's rights. Thank you for respecting the hard work of this author.

TABLE OF CONTENTS

What This Book is All About xv

Part One: Managing the Emotions xix

    1 Emotional Overwhelm 1

    2 Sadness 4

    3 Longing 8

    4 Fear 12

    5 Anxiety 15

    Grief Skill: The Habit of Deep Breathing 18

    6 Anger 19

    Quick Tips for Handling Grief Anger 24

    7 Guilt and Regret 25

    8 Numbness 30

    9 Depression 33

Part Two: Managing the Thoughts 39

    10 Mental Spinning 41

    11 Mental Fatigue 46

    12 Focus and Concentration Issues 50

    13 Memory Issues 56

14 Feeling Confused and Crazy 60

Part Three: Managing the Physical Impact 65
    15 Physical Symptoms 67
    16 Fatigue and Exhaustion 72
    17 Sleep Disturbances 75
    18 Eating and Weight 79
    19 Balance and Coordination 83
    20 Stress, Illness, and Disease 86
    21 Dreams and Nightmares 90
    22 Good Self-Care 94

Part Four: Managing the Spiritual Impact 99
    23 Questions, Questions, and More Questions 101
    24 Why? 105
    25 Anger with God 109
    26 Spiritual / Faith Relationships 113
    27 Spiritual Doubts and Faith Crises 117
    28 Spiritual Fatigue and Numbness 122
    29 Spiritual Growth 126

Part Five: Managing Relationships 131
    30 Changing Relationships 133
    31 Five People We Meet in Grief 136
    32 Disappearing People 142
    33 Unsupportive People 146
    34 Expectations 150
    35 Safe People 156
    36 Work Relationships 159

    37 Spouse and Partner Relationships ... 164
    38 Parenting in Grief ... 169
    39 Family Relationships ... 175
    40 Guarding Your Heart ... 179

Part Six: Managing the Future ... 183
    41 The Anticipated Future ... 185
    42 Lost Hopes and Dreams ... 189
    43 Future Grief Bursts ... 193
    44 Holidays and Special Times ... 198
    Ideas for Holidays and Special Occasions ... 202
    45 Identity Crisis ... 204
    46 Decision-Making ... 207
    47 Mission and Purpose ... 211
    48 Using Our Grief for Good ... 216

Concluding Thoughts ... 221

An Invitation To Make A Difference ... 223

Additional Grief Resources ... 225

Free On Gary's Website ... 227

A Request from the Author ... 229

About the Author ... 231

Acknowledgments ... 233

An Urgent Plea: Help Other Grieving Hearts ... 235

Thank you for purchasing the
Grieving the Write Way Journal and Workbook.

These pages are designed to be a companion
for you in your grief journey.

Please don't go through this workbook just once.

Pick it up again in six months or a year.

Come to it again and again.

Each time you will be at a different place.

You'll see your progress. You'll be encouraged.

And you'll find your hope has grown.

As a thanks, please accept this gift – a free eBook (PDF):

Grief: 9 Things I Wish I Had Known

Download yours today:

https://www.garyroe.com/grief-9-things-i-wish-i-had-known-ebook/

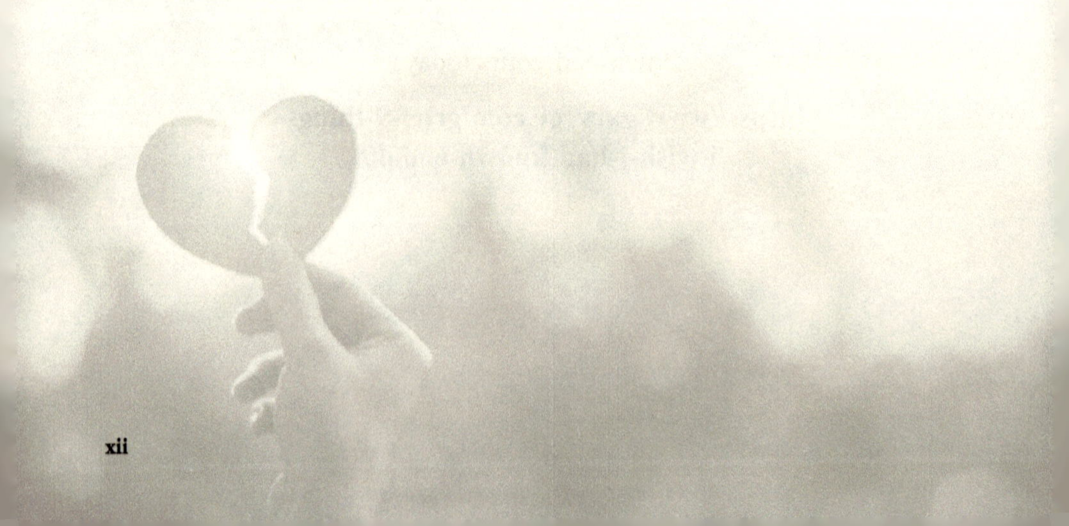

OTHER BOOKS BY GARY ROE

THE COMFORT SERIES

Comfort for Grieving Hearts: Hope and Encouragement in Times of Loss

Comfort for the Grieving Spouse's Heart: Hope and Healing After Losing Your Partner

Comfort for the Grieving Adult Child's Heart: Hope and Healing After Losing Your Parent

Comfort for the Grieving Parent's Heart: Hope and Healing After Losing Your Child

THE GOD AND GRIEF SERIES

Grief Walk: Experiencing God After the Loss of a Loved One

Widowed Walk: Experiencing God After the Loss of a Spouse

Orphaned Walk: Experiencing God After the Loss of a Parent

THE GOOD GRIEF SERIES

The Grief Guidebook: Common Questions, Compassionate Answers, Practical Suggestions

Aftermath: Picking Up the Pieces After a Suicide

Shattered: Surviving the Loss of a Child

Teen Grief: Caring for the Grieving Teenage Heart

Please Be Patient, I'm Grieving: How to Care for and Support the Grieving Heart

Heartbroken: Healing from the Loss of a Spouse

Surviving the Holidays Without You: Navigating Loss During Special Seasons

THE DIFFERENCE MAKER SERIES

Difference Maker: Overcoming Adversity and Turning Pain into Purpose, Every Day (Adult & Teen Editions)

Living on the Edge: How to Fight and Win the Battle for Your Mind and Heart (Adult & Teen Editions)

WHAT THIS BOOK IS ALL ABOUT

Your world has changed. Someone special is missing.

This loss hits you on all levels: emotional, mental, physical, spiritual, and relational. Your routine has been upended. Life for you is not business as usual.

How do you do this?

What does this loss mean for you?

Who are you now?

What's next?

MY PERSONAL HISTORY WITH WRITING AND GRIEF

I experienced multiple, traumatic losses in early childhood. By the time I was a teenager, I was slogging through each day carrying massive weights that I was unaware of.

Then I lost my dad. He dropped in front of me of a heart attack. He was a single dad and my one functional parent.

My grief burden was already massive. When this lightning bolt struck, I thought my life was over.

I was stunned.

I managed to stay functional. I went to school. I stayed on the swim team. I kept connecting with my friends. Because of previous losses, however, I already felt different from my peers. Now, I felt like I lived alone in some alternate universe.

One day I picked up a pencil and started writing. A poem materialized. I wasn't a poetry fan, but somehow it fit my mood that day.

The next day, I wrote another poem. A few days later, I penned another.

Emotion began to spill out as I wrote. I cried. I paced and talked to myself. I yelled and screamed.

Writing poetry opened an avenue for my heart to express its anguish. Sadness, confusion, anger, fear, anxiety, and guilt spewed out of me, one word at a time. I felt lousy but expressing myself felt good and relieving.

I continued writing poetry throughout high school. In college, I began to journal. When I was upset or frustrated, I found myself writing down what I was feeling and thinking.

Keeping a journal became a habit. Writing about what was happening in my heart and mind became a part of my daily routine. I continue this today.

I write in the morning, before the pressures and interruptions of the day begin their assault. I get to process what happened yesterday. I prepare myself for today.

As a hospice chaplain, grief specialist, and grief coach, I'm around death, loss, and heavy grief every day. I use writing to process and release the huge amount of pain that I hear and see.

Frankly, I don't know what I would do without writing as a way of processing life.

WRITING AND THE GRIEF PROCESS

Writing can play a massive part in the grief and healing process.

Writing steadies our hearts enough to express our emotions in a healthy and productive way.

Writing slows our spinning minds down enough to get our thoughts on paper and begin to process them.

Writing can enable us to consider the physical impact of grief on our bodies and help us decide what to do about it.

Writing gives us a safe place to express and process spiritual questions, doubts, and fears.

Writing allows us to share our frustrations about our relationships in an honest and uncensored manner.

Writing enables us to consider and work through our thoughts, wonderings, and fears about the future.

Writing can become a powerful habit that can help us navigate life in general. What we don't express stays locked in our hearts and often becomes some of the baggage that weighs us down.

Writing can be a tool which unveils hope. Hope is always here, but sometimes pain can blind us to it.

HOW THIS BOOK CAN HELP

This book is about you and the terrible loss you're enduring.

This book is about helping you express your heart, mind, and soul.

This book can aid you in tackling (in a sane and healthy way) all the changes that have been thrust upon you.

This book can assist you in navigating all the relational changes and upsets you're facing.

This book can help you honor your loved one as you grieve.

This book can help you see that you're not alone, you're not crazy, and that you will make it through this.

This book can help you take the next steps in your grief process, whatever they might be.

WELCOME TO GRIEVING THE WRITE WAY

So, welcome to the *Grieving the Write Way Journal and Workbook*. In the following pages, you'll get many opportunities to experience the benefits of writing about your loss and what's happening in your heart and mind.

As you move through the material, you'll find yourself getting more comfortable with journaling using prompts.

You'll discover how to use letters and stories to process losses and other life events.

You'll dabble in the creative process of writing poetry. Even if you're not a poetry fan, I'm hoping you'll be surprised and pleased by what you get out of it.

I'm glad you're here. Take the next step. Read on…and write.

PART ONE:

MANAGING THE EMOTIONS

Loss hits our hearts. Emotions rise from deep within us. These feelings are powerful and can hijack our lives.

Emotional overwhelm is common.

How do we deal with this?

This section is designed to help you process the tremendous emotional impact loss can have. As you read and write, breathe deeply from time to time. Express your heart, as best you can. Be as real and as honest as possible.

1

EMOTIONAL OVERWHELM

"My loss caused an emotional avalanche. I'm suffocating under the weight of it."

– Carl, after the death of his wife

After a loss, powerful emotions often surge up within us. Our feelings can be so intense that they begin to dominate our lives and routines.

Sadness, confusion, frustration, anger, guilt, fear, anxiety, and depression come at us like ocean waves. Some waves are smaller and easier to navigate than others. Some are powerful and temporarily knock us off our feet. Others might overwhelm us.

And the waves just keep coming. If we get a break, it's not for very long.

In our world, mood is king. How we feel in the present moment tends to govern what we do and how. After a loss, emotions tend to expand and take up more space. In grief, intense feelings can hijack us in an instant.

Feeling emotionally overwhelmed is common for grieving hearts.

Take a moment and list some of the feelings and emotions that you have experienced on your grief journey so far:

_____

_____

_____

_____

_____

_____

_____

Of these, which feelings have been the most challenging for you?

_____

_____

_____

_____

_____

_____

_____

_____

Writing Prompts:

Begin by completing the sentence and then free yourself to keep writing about whatever comes to mind.

"When I feel emotionally overwhelmed, I find myself wondering..."

_____
_____
_____
_____
_____
_____

"When I'm hijacked by my feelings, I tend to respond by..."

_____
_____
_____
_____
_____
_____

You may feel overwhelmed at times. That's okay. Try to be patient with yourself. Handle what you can, as you can. Take one moment, one step at a time.

2

SADNESS

"I have never known such sadness. It seems to cover everything."

– Sandy, after the loss of her daughter

Sadness is the most common and most prevalent of all the grief emotions. You've lost someone special. Sadness is a natural result.

Sadness can be like a stabbing pain to the heart. It can also feel like a constant, dull ache.

Our sadness can resemble a heavy cloud that seems to cover everything.

Processing the sadness within you and "getting it out" is important. Your sadness honors the one you lost. Expressing that sadness is one way of saying, "I love you."

How would you describe sadness? Try to write a simple definition:

_____

_____

_____

_____

_____

_____

_____

Think of some of the times you've felt sad since your loss. Describe one (or a couple) of these times:

_____

_____

_____

_____

_____

_____

_____

_____

Writing Prompts:

Begin by completing the sentence and then keep writing about whatever comes to mind.

"When I think about my loss, I feel sad about..."

_____

_____

_____

_____

_____

_____

_____

_____

_____

_____

_____

_____

_____

_____

_____

_____

_____

"When I feel sad about my loss, I usually..."

_____

Feeling sad is natural after a loss. Take your heart seriously and express your sadness in healthy ways. Your sadness is your heart saying, "I love you."

3

LONGING

"Her absence is like the sky, spread over everything."

— C.S. Lewis, A Grief Observed

When someone special dies or leaves, our hearts grieve. The pain of missing them can be great.

As time passes, we long to be with them. We want what we had. We're designed for relationship and connection, not for separation.

We long to see their face.

We long to hear their voice.

We long to touch them.

We long to be in their presence.

We long for everything we miss.

Everything seems to remind us of them. They are never far from our hearts and minds.

Expressing the longings within you is healthy and healing. Let your heart speak.

As you think about your loss, what do you sense your heart is longing for?

Writing Prompts:

Begin by completing the sentence and then write about whatever comes to mind.

"When I think of you, my heart longs to..."

_____
_____
_____
_____
_____
_____

"Today, I wish I could..."

_____
_____
_____
_____
_____
_____
_____
_____
_____

Memory Writing Exercise:

When you think about what you long for, what memories of your loved one come to mind?

Pick one memory that seems to be strongest in your heart today. Write about that memory below. Don't evaluate or edit. Just write. Let your heart express itself.

_____

_____

_____

_____

_____

_____

_____

_____

_____

_____

_____

_____

_____

When we lose someone, our hearts naturally long for the good we had. Expressing these longings is good, healthy, and healing. Let your heart speak.

4

FEAR

"I'm afraid of everything now. Terrified, actually."

– Stephanie, after the death of her two sons

Immediately after a loss, we're in shock. We're stunned and perhaps even immobilized. As hours and days go by, a stark reality begins to dawn on us: If this can happen, what else might?

We wonder what's ahead. How are we going to do this? What's next?

A sense of powerlessness can emerge. On some level, we become aware that anything can happen to anyone at any time. Fear begins to surface.

Fear can be powerful. At times, it might threaten to overwhelm us and take over our lives. Fear can become the unseen motivator behind our thoughts and decisions.

Fear is often a part of the grief process. As such, it needs to be acknowledged, identified, and expressed. As we're honest about what's happening inside us, we can then process and release it over time.

Look inside your heart. What fears are lurking there? What are you afraid of?

List your fears here:

_____
_____
_____
_____
_____
_____

Of the fears listed above, which ones seem to disturb you the most?

_____
_____
_____
_____
_____
_____
_____
_____
_____
_____
_____

Writing Prompts:

Begin by completing the sentence and then keep writing about whatever comes to mind.

"Since my loss, I find myself fearful that..."

_____
_____
_____
_____
_____
_____

"When I'm afraid, I typically respond by..."

_____
_____
_____
_____
_____
_____

Fear is common in grief. Acknowledging and expressing fears as they arise is important and healthy.

5

ANXIETY

"I'm anxious all the time now. Sometimes, I even forget to breathe."

– Cassandra, after the loss of her mom

When we experience loss, our anxiety level automatically rises.

Our lives have been shaken. Our personal worlds have been altered. This is shocking and unnerving. Anxiety is a natural result.

We can experience increased nervousness. Many have anxiety or panic attacks. We feel worried, fearful, and shaky inside.

Managing grief anxiety can be a challenge. The first key to this is remembering that we are not alone. High anxiety is natural and extremely common for those on the grief journey.

Breathing deeply is a simple grief skill that can aid us greatly in handling the natural anxiety that comes. See the end of this chapter for a detailed description.

What do you tend to get anxious about? Make a list. Be as specific as you can.

___

When you feel anxious, what do you tend to do next? How do you handle that anxiety?

___

Writing Prompts:

Begin by completing the sentence and then express freely what comes to your heart and mind.

"Since my loss, I notice that I'm more anxious about..."

_____

_____

_____

_____

_____

_____

"When anxiety strikes, I wish I could respond by..."

_____

_____

_____

_____

_____

_____

Handling grief anxiety can be a bit like riding a roller coaster. Acknowledging the anxiety and then processing it well is healthy for your heart and mind.

GRIEF SKILL

THE HABIT OF DEEP BREATHING

The habit of deep breathing is an important grief processing skill. Those who practice it regularly have found it extremely helpful in managing the volatile thoughts and emotions that are part of the grief journey.

Breathe in deeply through your nose and then out through your mouth. As an EMT friend of mine says, "Smell the roses, blow out the candle." This activates your parasympathetic nervous system and brings a calming effect to your brain and body.

Breathe deeply and slowly for at least a couple of minutes. Focus as much as possible on your breathing. Close your eyes if necessary.

Consider practicing deep breathing twice a day - once at the beginning of your day and again at the end. As you do this, you're training your mind and body to respond to the intense grief bursts that will come. The more you practice this, the more of a habit deep breathing will become and the easier you'll be able to initiate it when you need it.

Before you read on, practice deep breathing for a few more minutes. Again, this simple skill can be massively beneficial during this time of loss. And the good news is that anyone can do it, anytime, anywhere.

Breathe.

6

ANGER

"I know anger is a part of grief, but I don't like it. I don't know what to do with it, either."

– Brandon, after the death of his brother

Anger is a natural grief emotion. It comes to almost all grieving hearts.

Anger is a powerful emotion. We see its negative effects in the world and in our own past. Many of us struggle with how to best handle it.

Anger itself is simply an emotion. As such, it is neutral. How we deal with and express our anger, however, can be either positive and healing or negative and hurtful.

Anger takes many forms in grief. Upset and frustration. Impatience and irritability. Agitation and aggressive driving. Rages and explosions. Silence and depression. Unhealthy habits and addictions.

We're wired for connection. We're made to love and be loved. When someone special dies or departs, our hearts are broken. Though we know death and separation happen, it all feels wrong somehow. Anger is a natural result.

Acknowledging your anger is the first step. Finding healthy ways to express it and "let it out" will be important in your grief process.

When do you typically get angry?

_____

_____

_____

_____

_____

_____

_____

How do you usually express that anger?

_____

_____

_____

_____

_____

_____

_____

_____

Writing Prompts:

Use the following prompts to begin to process your grief anger. Be as honest as you can. Write whatever comes to mind.

"Since my loss, I've found myself angry about..."

_____
_____
_____
_____
_____
_____
_____

"When it comes to managing anger, I wish I could..."

_____
_____
_____
_____
_____
_____
_____

Letter Writing Exercise

There are times when writing a letter can be extremely helpful and healing. In this case, consider writing a letter to someone you are angry with. Of course, this is a letter you will never send.

Picture the person in front of you. Write about what you're thinking and feeling. Resist the temptation to hold back or censor yourself. Express yourself freely. The goal here is to "get the anger out."

_____
_____
_____
_____
_____
_____
_____
_____
_____
_____
_____
_____
_____
_____

Managing grief anger is difficult. Be patient with yourself. Acknowledge the anger when it comes. Then focus on "getting it out" in healthy ways.

QUICK TIPS FOR HANDLING GRIEF ANGER

- Practice the art of deep breathing. The more you make this a habit, the more beneficial it will be when anger rises within you. See yourself breathing in calm and breathing out your anger. See the end of chapter five for more info on this important grief processing skill.

- Exercise. Regular, moderate exercise appropriate for your age and health is extremely helpful in managing anger.

- Talk about your anger when it comes. Talk out loud to yourself when alone. Share and vent with someone safe who will just listen.

- Punch a pillow. Walk around punching the air.

- Scream and yell. Scream into a pillow. Yell in a private place where you won't be disturbed.

- Once you've processed the anger, see yourself releasing it. Picture the anger in your hand and make a fist. When you're ready, open your hand and release that anger.

- Imagine your anger is a balloon you're holding onto. After you express that anger and "get it out," see yourself releasing the balloon. See your anger drifting up and away from you.

- Limit your exposure to unhelpful people and influences. You don't need extra challenges right now.

7

GUILT AND REGRET

"When I look back, all I see are mistakes."

– Ben, after the loss of his son

After a close loss, guilt often comes knocking.

We naturally go back and think about what we could have done or should have done. We wince at some of what we did or didn't say or do. Our imperfections, mistakes, and perceived failures begin to haunt us.

"What if..." and "If only..." scenarios play over and over again in our minds and hearts.

Many find it helpful to make a distinction between guilt and regret.

Regret says, "I wish I had or hadn't..." and "If I had known what I know now, I would have..." We all have regrets. Regrets are natural and reasonable.

Guilt says, "It's my fault. I'm responsible for what happened. I caused this." Guilt is an accuser. It points its crooked finger at us and sneers, "You did this."

When it comes to your own heart, try distinguishing your regrets from guilt.

Regrets:

"With regard to my loss, I wish I had..."

_____
_____
_____
_____
_____
_____
_____

"With regard to my loss, I wish I hadn't..."

_____
_____
_____
_____
_____
_____
_____

"If I had known then what I know now, I would have..."

_____
_____

_____

_____

_____

_____

_____

Guilt:

"With regard to my loss, I feel it's my fault that..."

_____

_____

_____

_____

_____

_____

"When I feel guilty, I usually..."

_____

_____

_____

_____

_____

Most grieving hearts tussle with guilt at some point. Distinguishing between guilt and regret can be helpful.

Letter Writing Exercise

Write a letter to yourself from the loved one or friend you lost. What would they say to you about your regrets and feelings of guilt? Don't overthink this. Just write...

_____

_____

_____

_____

_____

_____

_____

_____

_____

_____

_____

_____

_____

_____

_____

_____

8

NUMBNESS

"Sometimes, I feel nothing – nothing at all."

– Liz, after the death of her husband

Grief can be emotionally overwhelming. None of us can handle the full weight of loss all the time. Just like an electric circuit, our hearts can get overloaded. Our feelers can temporarily shut down.

Most grieving hearts experience a sense of numbness from time to time in their grief journey. This is natural and even healthy. Numbness, though it can be disturbing and uncomfortable, can help protect our hearts and minds from damage. We need breaks from grief's grinding intensity.

As with other aspects of grief, acknowledging what's happening inside us is the first step to processing it.

If you have felt numb in your grief journey, describe what that was like.

When you feel numb, what do you typically do? How does this affect your life and routine?

Writing Prompts:

Use the following prompts to begin to process this emotional numbness. Write whatever comes to mind.

"When I'm numb - when I feel nothing - I wonder..."

_____
_____
_____
_____
_____
_____

"When I'm numb, I'm most concerned about..."

_____
_____
_____
_____
_____
_____

Feeling numb is something experienced by many grieving hearts. Be kind to yourself. Accept yourself where you are, as you are.

9

DEPRESSION

"The risk of love is loss, and the price of loss is grief - but the pain of grief is only a shadow when compared with the pain of never risking love."

- Hilary Stanton Zunin

The emotional onslaught after a loss can be heavy. We experience sadness, frustration, anger, fear, anxiety, and guilt. At times, we might feel nothing at all. Our world has changed. We sense we are changing. We don't like this new life. All of this put together can be depressing.

Most grieving hearts experience some depression on their grief journey. In most cases, this depression is temporary and situational. In others words, most of us feel depressed for a period of time directly as a result of our loss.

How do you know if you're depressed? Here are some typical signs of temporary depression that grievers can experience:

- An ongoing sense of sadness

- Frequent bouts of crying

- Poor concentration

- Lack of motivation

- Loss of pleasure

- Withdrawing from usual or normal activities
- Loneliness and increased social isolation
- Hopelessness

Temporary, situational depression can come and go throughout the grief process.

Rather than hiding this, being intentional about expressing and processing this depression is crucial. We need to open the spillways of our grief reservoir and "let the depression out."

If you've felt depressed since your loss, describe what that was like. What did you feel, think, and experience?

_____

_____

_____

_____

_____

When you're in the midst of temporary depression, what do you think would be helpful to you?

_____

_____

_____

_____

_____

_____

_____

_____

_____

Writing Prompts:

Use the prompts below to express more of your heart and mind regarding some of the grief depression you have experienced.

"I feel depressed when I think of…"

_____
_____
_____
_____
_____
_____

"When I think about depression, I hope that…"

_____
_____
_____
_____
_____
_____
_____
_____
_____

Letter Writing Exercise

Write a letter to someone safe that you trust. You won't send this letter, of course, but having the recipient in mind will help you write. Think of a time that you felt depressed. Tell them about it.

Experiencing some temporary situational depression is common in the grief process. These heavy feelings and thoughts are natural during the grief journey. Be kind to yourself. Process your grief depression as it comes.

PART TWO:

MANAGING THE THOUGHTS

Grief hits not only our hearts but our minds as well.

Our thoughts spin. Our brains become foggy.

We can't focus or concentrate like usual. Memory issues can surface. We can feel like we're losing our minds.

In this section, we're going to explore the mental impact a close loss can have. Take your time as you move through these pages. Express what's happening inside you. Be kind to yourself along the way.

10

MENTAL SPINNING

"My thoughts go round and round like a hamster on a wheel."

– Jeff, after the loss of his father

Our minds move with amazing speed. When we're grieving, our thoughts can bounce all over the place. Most grieving hearts experience their share of mental spinning.

We wonder about this or that. Concerns swirl around us. Our to-do list is a mile long. Our thoughts go round and round. Our brains feel like a hamster on a wheel. Our minds are moving but our thoughts don't seem to be going anywhere.

Writing can be terrifically helpful here. Our hands (or fingers if we're typing) move much slower than our brains. When we write, we force our minds to slow down enough to express some of what's happening inside. In some ways, writing gives our circling, bouncing thoughts a place to land.

Have you experienced some mental spinning since your loss? Describe what this is like for you.

_____
_____
_____
_____
_____
_____

How do you usually respond when your mind spins?

_____
_____
_____
_____
_____
_____
_____
_____

Writing Prompts:

Use the prompts below to help process your spinning thoughts. Free yourself to express wherever your mind takes you.

"If I made a list of my spinning thoughts, I would definitely include..."

_____
_____
_____
_____
_____
_____
_____

"When my mind spins, the thoughts that concern me the most are..."

_____
_____
_____
_____
_____
_____

Mental spinning is natural and common for grieving hearts. Do your best to process your mental carousel. Consider having a sheet of paper or notepad handy for these times. When your mind spins, begin writing your thoughts.

Over time, "getting the grief out" in this way will be relieving and healing.

Memory Writing Exercise:

When your mind spins, are there particular memories of your loved one that surface? Briefly list some of those memories here:

_____
_____
_____
_____
_____

Pick one of these memories. Write about that memory below. Write whatever comes to mind. Let your heart express itself.

_____
_____
_____
_____
_____
_____
_____
_____

11

MENTAL FATIGUE

"I can't think. I can barely lift my head."

– Kayla, after the loss of her best friend

We said previously that at times our brains can feel like a hamster on a wheel. Our minds go, and go, and go. Thoughts circle around and bounce about. The speed and constancy of all this mental activity can be exhausting.

Mental fatigue is the natural result, and it is common in grief.

Some grievers report that their heads feel heavy. Others talk about zoning out or having difficulty thinking at times. Some have trouble finding the right words on occasion. Still others state that they feel robotic and like they're not really there but just going through the motions.

Many simply say, "My brain feels tired."

Have you experienced any of these things? If so, describe what mental fatigue is like for you.

___

When your brain feels tired, what do you typically do? Do you wish you could do something different? If so, what?

___

Letter Writing Exercise:

Write a letter to the friend or loved one you lost. Describe your mental fatigue to them. What are you thinking and feeling during these times?

Be as specific as you can. Let your mind go. Write whatever comes.

_____
_____
_____
_____
_____
_____
_____
_____
_____
_____
_____
_____
_____
_____
_____

Brain fatigue is natural and common on the grief journey. When you write, you give your worn synapses a place to rest. Writing can be a form of exercise that helps "get the fatigue out."

12

FOCUS AND CONCENTRATION ISSUES

"My thoughts are like a thousand butterflies randomly flitting in every possible direction."

– Karla, after the loss of her dad

―――⧼⧽―――

After a heavy loss occurs, grief begins to gobble up our internal real estate. Grief thoughts and emotions surface and flood our minds and hearts. Naturally, our ability to focus and concentrate will be affected.

Perhaps we notice that we're not as quick or sharp mentally. Maybe we find our minds wandering more than usual. We seem to tire more easily. We're not as resilient. We miss details. We neglect certain things without even realizing it. We make more mistakes.

Of course, this affects our work performance. We might be able to fake it for a while, but eventually it becomes clear we're not at our best right now. If others are depending on us and how well we perform, this adds additional stress to our already heavy load.

Many grievers feel like they're not all there. The reality is that grief is taking up a lot of our internal space and there is simply less mental energy left to do life right now.

Have you had more trouble focusing and concentrating since your loss? Do you sense your work is being affected? Describe what this has been like for you so far.

_____

_____

_____

_____

_____

_____

When we have difficulty focusing, many of us are hard on ourselves. We beat ourselves up mentally when we're already down. When you notice you're having trouble concentrating, what do you say to yourself? Is what you say to yourself helpful?

_____

_____

_____

_____

_____

_____

_____

_____

Writing Prompts:

Use the prompts below to write about this issue. Resist the temptation to overanalyze. Just write whatever comes to mind.

"I notice I have trouble concentrating when..."

_____
_____
_____
_____
_____
_____
_____
_____
_____
_____

"When I have trouble focusing, I tend to..."

_____
_____
_____

"I think it might help if I…"

Poetry Writing Exercise:

Using the following list of words, try writing a poem about the focus and concentration issues you've faced since your loss. Feel free to use any other words you wish in addition to these. Don't be concerned about rhyme, meter, or composition. Free your mind and heart to use these words to express what you think and feel.

*Heart   Mind   Brain   Focus   Concentrate   Wander
Wonder   Think   Head   Thoughts   Trouble*

_____
_____
_____
_____
_____
_____
_____
_____
_____
_____
_____
_____
_____
_____

Most grieving hearts experience some concentration issues on their grief journey. As you process your grief and "get it out" in healthy ways, most likely your mental focus will return. Right now, your brain is being squeezed by grief. Be patient and do what you can to accept yourself along the way.

13

MEMORY ISSUES

"I think I'm losing my mind."

– Aaron, after the death of his wife

"I think I'm losing it," is a common statement among those on the grief journey. Memory issues are often part of the mental impact of a close loss.

We can't remember where we put things. We forget why we came into the room. We blip out in the middle of a sentence and can't seem to find the right words. We miss appointments. We can't recall what we did last week, yesterday, or even an hour ago.

These brain blips can be disconcerting to many. We wonder what's happening. Is something wrong? Are we developing dementia? Do we have a tumor? Are we going crazy?

Loss and the resulting grief naturally upset our usual balance. Simply put, we have less available mental space right now. We're mentally overcrowded. Our brains can't hold it all.

In other words, increased forgetfulness is natural, reasonable, and common in the grief process.

Have you noticed you're more forgetful since your loss? Write about this. Give some examples.

_____
_____
_____
_____
_____
_____
_____
_____

When you realize you've forgotten something, how do you react?

_____
_____
_____
_____
_____
_____
_____
_____

Writing Prompts:

New or increased memory problems can be frustrating and unnerving. Use the prompts below to process this.

"When I forget something, I wonder (or worry) about..."

_____

_____

_____

_____

_____

_____

_____

"With regard to my memory, I think I could help myself by..."

_____

_____

_____

_____

_____

_____
_____
_____
_____
_____
_____
_____
_____
_____
_____
_____
_____
_____
_____
_____
_____

Loss hits our entire being, including our minds. With all the whirlwind of emotions and change, it's natural for some thoughts to get lost along the way. You're not superhuman. You're hurting and grieving. Give yourself a break.

As you continue to process your grief in healthy ways, most likely your memory will bounce back over time.

14

FEELING CONFUSED AND CRAZY

"I feel confused. In fact, I feel crazy sometimes."

– Barb, after the loss of her life partner

When a close loss occurs, our personal worlds are permanently altered. In some sense, everything is different now.

We look around us, however, and everything looks much the same. The rest of the world zips along much as before. It's like we're now in some alternate reality looking in from the outside. Weird. Surreal. This is frustrating and confusing.

Feeling confused or even a little crazy is common for those of us on the grief journey.

The truth is that we're not crazy, but life seems crazy now compared to before. It's like someone rearranged everything overnight and we woke up in a different world. Nothing feels the same.

Our hearts and minds are desperately trying to process and make sense of all this. Feeling a bit unhinged every now and then is a natural result.

Have you felt a little crazy in your grief process so far? Describe some examples.

_____
_____
_____
_____
_____
_____

When you're feeling a little crazy, what do you typically do? What do you sense you're telling yourself? Is it helpful?

_____
_____
_____
_____
_____
_____
_____
_____
_____
_____

Letter Writing Exercise

Imagine yourself to be a detached observer watching you on your grief journey. Write yourself a letter from this perspective. What would a detached, outside observer say to you about "feeling crazy" during this time?

Again, don't overthink this. Write whatever comes to mind. Resist the temptation to edit as you go. Just write.

_____
_____
_____
_____
_____
_____
_____
_____
_____
_____
_____
_____
_____
_____

Feeling a little unhinged is common for grieving hearts. The overwhelming amount of change that flows from our loss can be staggering.

Breathe deeply. You're not crazy, but loss and the resulting grief can make you wonder.

PART THREE:

MANAGING THE PHYSICAL IMPACT

When we lose someone special, our bodies feel the shock.

We can begin to experience weird or exacerbated physical symptoms and more frequent illnesses.

The constant stress of all the change occurring in our lives can whittle away at our health.

The daily grind of grief can wear us out.

In this section, we'll delve into the frustrating and often disturbing physical impact grief can have.

15

PHYSICAL SYMPTOMS

Loss hits our entire being. Our bodies feel the shock too.

As a result, many on the grief journey experience new or exacerbated physical symptoms.

Headaches, migraines, muscle tension, joint pain, and back pain. Stomach distress, gastrointestinal issues, nausea, dizziness, and vertigo. Racing heartbeat, palpitations, chest pressure, chest pain, arrhythmias, and shortness of breath. Fatigue, exhaustion, insomnia, colds, flus, illnesses, and infections. The list goes on and on.

Loss can have stunning physical impact. Our health can wobble and shake under the ongoing weight of grief. Taking care of ourselves becomes more important than ever.

Physical symptoms like these can be worrisome and frightening. If we're concerned, we need to reach out to a medical professional and get checked out. Amid all the upheaval, we need to know we're okay. Reassurance is priceless when we're grieving.

Have you experienced any new or exacerbated symptoms or health issues since your loss? If so, list them here.

_____

_____

_____

_____

_____

When you experience these physical issues, how does it affect your daily life?

_____

_____

_____

_____

_____

_____

_____

_____

_____

Writing Prompts:

Use the following prompts to process what's happening to you physically. Let your mind go where it wants to. Write freely.

"When I think of the symptoms I'm experiencing (or have experienced), I find myself wondering about…"

_____

_____

_____

_____

_____

_____

"Amid all the stress and change, I could take better care of myself by…"

_____

_____

_____

_____

_____

_____

_____

Poetry Writing Exercise:

Using the following words, try writing a poem about the symptoms you've experienced since your loss. Try not to be overly concerned about whether your poem rhymes or what it looks like. Let your heart express what's happening inside you.

Heart   Body   Afraid   Strange   Pain
Grief   Loss   Time   Health

_____

_____

_____

_____

_____

_____

_____

_____

_____

_____

_____

_____

_____

Many grieving hearts encounter frustrating and troubling physical symptoms. Breathe deeply. Reach out to your physician for reassurance and input. Do what you can to take good care of yourself.

16

FATIGUE AND EXHAUSTION

The number one physical symptom reported by those in heavy grief is fatigue.

Loss hits us. Grief invades. Our emotions go wacky. Our minds spin and bounce. Managing all the change is draining.

Grief saps our strength. Our capacities are stretched and squeezed. Our worlds have been suddenly altered, and yet our responsibilities have not diminished. We're stunned, but life moves on and drags us along with it.

Exhaustion is commonplace. As one grieving heart said, "Even chewing my food takes Herculean effort."

Life is demanding and busy. Most of us are tired most of the time. Loss and grief rocket our fatigue to new heights. Now, just getting through the day is a huge accomplishment.

Describe the fatigue you've experienced in your grief process. Be as detailed as possible.

_____
_____
_____
_____
_____
_____
_____

When fatigue hits, what do you wish you could do?

_____
_____
_____
_____
_____
_____
_____
_____
_____

Writing Prompts:

Use the following prompts to write more about grief exhaustion.

"When fatigue hits, some of the things that are not helpful to me are..."

_____

_____

_____

_____

_____

_____

"When I'm exhausted, some things I can do to take care of myself are..."

_____

_____

_____

_____

_____

_____

_____

Fatigue and exhaustion are common in grief. Your body is feeling the weight of your loss. Your body is sending you messages. Something huge has happened. Someone special is missing.

Breathe deeply. Accept yourself as you are at present. Do what you can to express your grief in healthy ways.

17

SLEEP DISTURBANCES

"Grief is the price we pay for love."

- Queen Elizabeth II

Most grieving hearts struggle with sleep disturbances of some kind. Our lives have been upended. Our emotions, thoughts, and bodies are being shaken. It makes sense that our sleep would be disturbed too.

We have trouble getting to sleep. In the quiet of the night, our minds kick into high gear. We replay the past and our loss. We wonder and worry. Emotions surge up within us.

We have trouble staying asleep. We toss and turn. Perhaps we have dreams of our loved one, or even nightmares. We wake up trembling.

We wake up tired. It's as if our minds and hearts were working all night long. Perhaps we wonder if we really slept at all.

It's been said that sleep deprivation is the most basic form of torture. We heal when we sleep. Good rest is essential to good health. At a time when we need it the most, restful sleep seems to elude us.

How has your sleep been since your loss? What changes have you experienced that are different from your norm?

_____
_____
_____
_____
_____
_____

Describe a typical night from the time you go to bed until you get up.

_____
_____
_____
_____
_____
_____
_____
_____
_____
_____

Writing Prompts:

Use the following prompts to process this more.

"When I think of going to bed at night, I find myself thinking and feeling..."

_____

_____

_____

_____

_____

_____

"When I think about things that might help with my sleep, I think of..."

_____

_____

_____

_____

_____

Altered sleep patterns are a common result of a heavy loss. As you continue to process your grief in healthy ways, chances are your sleep will change over time.

Now is not forever. Be kind to yourself. Do what you can to promote better rest during this time.

Memory Writing Exercise:

When your mind is spinning at night and you can't sleep, are there certain memories of your loved one that surface repeatedly? Name these repetitive thoughts and list them below.

_____

_____

_____

_____

_____

_____

Pick one memory of the memories above. Write about this memory below. Express what's happening in your mind and heart.

_____

_____

_____

_____

_____

_____

_____

_____

_____

18

EATING AND WEIGHT

When loss strikes, if affects every part of life. This includes how and what we eat.

Grief tends to dull the senses. Food doesn't taste the same now. Many don't feel hungry and forget to eat. Some don't feel thirsty and don't hydrate well. Our clothes begin to feel loose and baggy. We're losing weight.

Others eat for comfort. We might be drawn to carbs and sugar. If we did this before, we will most likely do this even more while grieving. We can begin to gain weight and feel even worse.

We need good nutrition now more than ever. Yet eating well tends to be a challenge. Healthy eating often takes more effort, planning, and preparation. The more life squeezes us, the more we opt for the easy and convenient.

Eating well is normally challenging in our busy world. We have to make an intentional, ongoing choice to pursue personal wellness. When grieving, these choices can be even more difficult.

Have you noticed changes in your eating habits since your loss? Describe them.

_____
_____
_____
_____
_____
_____
_____

On a scale of 1 to 10, with 10 being the best possible, how would you rate your nutritional intake and eating habits? Describe why you chose this number.

_____
_____
_____
_____
_____
_____
_____
_____

Writing Prompts:

Use these prompts to process this issue of eating and weight a bit more. Don't hold back. Write whatever comes to mind.

"When it comes to food and my weight, I feel..."

_____

_____

_____

_____

_____

_____

_____

_____

_____

"When it comes to food and my weight, I would like to be able to..."

_____

_____

_____

_____

_____

"When I'm ready, one small step I could take toward greater wellness is…"

Your taste buds are feeling the loss too. Be kind to yourself. As you see things you sense need to change, make small adjustments. The grief walk can only be taken one step at a time.

19

BALANCE AND COORDINATION

After a heavy loss, many become more accident-prone. We stumble. We trip over our own feet. We bump into things and people. We cut ourselves while shaving or chopping vegetables. We burn ourselves while cooking. We shut our fingers in doors. We get injured more easily.

We drop things. We spill drinks and food. We drive differently. We can't seem to park straight. Our depth perception is off. Our balance is not what it was.

Many grieving hearts experience balance and coordination issues. We can wonder if something is wrong with us physically. This is incredibly frustrating, but natural and common.

If we're concerned, the best thing is to consult our physician and get checked out. A little reassurance can be hugely comforting. We're already dealing with enough uncertainty as it is.

Most of the time, our coordination and balance troubles will be short-lived. As we process our grief in healthy ways, our current accident-proneness will recede into the background over time.

Have you noticed you're more accident-prone during this time of loss? Describe this.

___

Is there anything you sense you can do to reduce accidents and injuries on your grief journey? Try to list a few things.

___

Writing Prompts:

Use the following prompts to think more about any balance or coordination challenges you're having.

"When I have an accident of some kind, I feel..."

_____

_____

_____

_____

_____

_____

"While grieving and being more accident-prone, I can be kind to myself by..."

_____

_____

_____

_____

_____

_____

Grief expresses itself in many ways, including coordination and balance issues. Slowing down a bit and taking our time may help. Accepting ourselves along the way is important. The world is hard on grieving hearts. We need to give ourselves mercy, grace, and a lot of kindness.

20

STRESS, ILLNESS, AND DISEASE

Loss is a natural stress-producer. The grief process is packed with change. Change, even good change, is stressful. We lived stressful lives before. Now, the grinding pressure of grief stress can be unrelenting.

Over time, stress begins to suppress our immune systems. Many report more frequent colds and illnesses. Some things our bodies were able to keep in check before may begin to surface. Some can even develop stress-related diseases as a result of all the upheaval.

Can grief make a person sick? Yes, it can.

Again, checking in with our physician during a time of loss is important. We need their input and advice. We need their care, reassurance, and guidance.

Reducing what stress we can is crucial. Most of us tend to be hard on ourselves. We don't need that kind of pressure when we're already down. Being kind to ourselves and taking good care of ourselves need to become our new priorities.

Has your stress level increased since your loss? How so?

How does your grief stress seem to be manifesting itself physically?

Letter Writing Exercise

Become a detached observer of yourself. See yourself under all the weight of this grief stress. Notice how it's affecting you.

Write a letter to yourself. Consider the following things as topics in your letter:

- How you see grief stress affecting your life.
- What you would say to yourself to express concern, kindness, and hope.
- What you would tell yourself to do that might help.

Write freely. Resist the temptation to edit. Write whatever comes to mind.

_____

_____

_____

_____

_____

_____

_____

_____

_____

_____

_____

_____

Grief is incredibly stressful. Reduce what stress you can. Make self-care your priority.

21

DREAMS AND NIGHTMARES

During our sleep, we tend to process things our minds can't get to during the day. Our subconscious mind is always awake. Our dreams and nightmares can often be a reflection of this.

There's always more happening inside us than we're aware of. When we sleep, many of these subconscious things bubble up to the surface. Just as sleep can promote physical healing, it can also give us a needed opportunity to process what we can't when we're awake.

Many grieving hearts have dreams of those they've lost. Some dreams may be reassuring. Others may cause us to question this or that. Some dreams bring joy, while others stir our longings.

Some grievers have nightmares along the way. These are often related to traumatic events and mental images (real or imagined). If we feel personally responsible for some part of our loss, this can weigh heavily on us and express itself during our sleep.

Not everyone has dreams of their loved one or friend. This can be disturbing. We can feel like we've forgotten them somehow. We long to see them again, and dreams are one way we can feel more connected.

Processing dreams (or the lack of them) and nightmares further is important.

Have you had dreams and / or nightmares since your loss? If so, describe what they are typically like. If you haven't had any dreams, describe how you feel about this.

_____

_____

_____

_____

_____

_____

_____

_____

If you could write your own script for a dream, what would it include?

_____

_____

_____

_____

_____

_____

_____

_____

Writing Prompts:

Try processing your dreams and / or nightmares further by using these prompts.

"One dream (or nightmare) I particularly remember is..." (If you don't have dreams, try this prompt: "I wish I could have a dream where...").

_____

_____

_____

_____

_____

_____

"After a dream (or nightmare), I find myself wondering..."

_____

_____

_____

_____

_____

_____

_____

Poetry Writing Exercise:

Try writing a poem about your dreams using the words below. Free yourself to express what you think and feel.

*Dream   Sleep   Awake   Remember   Heart
Mind   Wonder   Grief*

Our subconscious mind is always active. Dreams or nightmares about the one we've lost are common. Continue to process these as they come.

22

GOOD SELF-CARE

"Grief is like the ocean; it comes on waves ebbing and flowing. Sometimes the water is calm, and sometimes it is overwhelming. All we can do is learn to swim."

- Vicki Harrison

Self-care is always a priority. While grieving, taking good care of ourselves is even more imperative.

In times of heavy stress, however, self-care is often neglected. In times of loss, we marshal our energies toward getting things done and fulfilling our responsibilities. Life seems to require even more energy and effort than it did before.

We find ourselves in a quandary. Self-care puts gas back in our tank, but it feels like there's not enough in our tank to pursue adequate self-care.

Good self-care is always a choice. As such, we often have to choose pursuing personal wellness over something else. We need to resist constantly giving way to the tyranny of the urgent. We need to put (and keep) first things first.

The greatest gift we can give to those around us is the healthiest us possible. This benefits everyone. This also honors those we've lost. Putting self-care at the top of our priority list is one way of saying "I love you" to both our loved one and those around us.

How has this loss affected your self-care? Describe this.

_____

_____

_____

_____

_____

_____

_____

When you think of self-care, what kinds of things come to mind? List them.

_____

_____

_____

_____

_____

_____

_____

_____

_____

Writing Prompts:

Use these prompts to process more about self-care and pursuing personal wellness while grieving.

"When it comes to self-care, I tend to be pretty good at..."

_____

_____

_____

_____

_____

_____

"When it comes to taking care of myself, I tend to struggle with..."

_____

_____

_____

_____

_____

_____

_____

_____

_____

"I believe that good self-care is important because..."

_____

_____

_____

_____

_____

_____

_____

_____

_____

"When it comes to taking care of myself and pursuing personal wellness, I think my next step is..." (and describe how you would do this).

_____

_____

_____

_____

_____

_____

Nutrition, hydration, exercise, and good rest all play a massive role in personal wellness. Getting around safe, healthy people and limiting your exposure to unhelpful influences is extremely important. Self-care, like everything else on the grief road, is a journey that we can only take one step at a time.

You are unique in human history. There's never been another person exactly like you, even if you're a twin. You matter deeply. We need you.

PART FOUR:

MANAGING THE SPIRITUAL IMPACT

In the previous sections, we processed some ways loss has affected us emotionally, mentally, and physically.

In this section, we'll be exploring the spiritual impact of loss.

We're relational beings at our core. When someone we love and care about departs, our souls can shake.

Perhaps we begin to question things we were sure about before. We can experience new doubts, fears, and even a faith crisis.

We end up living out what we really believe deep inside. Taking our souls seriously in the grief process is crucial to good self-care and to healing.

23

QUESTIONS, QUESTIONS, AND MORE QUESTIONS

When a heavy loss strikes our lives, our hearts are shaken. Soon, questions of all kinds begin to surface. Many of these questions have spiritual roots to them.

- "How did this happen? How *could* this happen?"

- "What do I do? How do I handle this?"

- "What's next? What does this mean for me?"

- "Who is responsible for this? Couldn't someone have done something to change or prevent this?"

- "Where was God? How does He fit into all this?"

- "If things like this happen, what's it all for? What's the meaning and point of life anyway?"

Some questions might be disturbing to us. Other questions may have no answers. Yet our hearts must ask the questions. We want to know. Our minds search for answers. Our hearts are squirming under the pain of our loss.

As with the rest of the grieving process, expressing what's happening inside us is helpful, relieving, and healing over time. We need to "get it out." Our soul questions need to be aired and expressed.

What questions have surfaced in your mind and heart since your loss? List them here.

Writing Prompts:

Use these prompts to process these questions further. Don't hold back or censor yourself. Write freely whatever comes to your mind and heart.

"Of all the questions that have surfaced in me, the questions I find myself asking over and over are..."

_____

_____

_____

_____

_____

_____

_____

"If I had to describe what my heart and soul are saying through these questions, I would say..."

_____

_____

_____

_____

_____

Being aware of and expressing your heart-soul questions is an important part of your grief process. These wonderings run deep. Letting them surface, getting them out, and accepting yourself along the way will be helpful.

24

WHY?

Of all the questions running around in our hearts and souls, "Why?" tends to be the deepest and the most perplexing.

"Why did this happen? Why them? Why me? Why us? Why this way? Why now? Why?"

Though "Why?" might be the question we want an answer to the most, answers are hard to come by. We're not perfect and we can't know everything. We're not in control. We're limited and there are things we simply can't know. Even if we knew the answer to our why questions, would we be emotionally satisfied?

Chances are, no matter what answer we come up with, it will feel hollow. The reality is we're missing our loved one. We want them back. We wish they were still here. We're hurting.

Though we get no satisfying answers, our why questions are important. We must express them. As we air these questions, we can begin to process the thoughts and emotions behind them. This leads to healing, adjustment, recovery, and growth over time.

What kind of why questions have your heart and soul been asking? List them here. Be as specific as possible.

_____

_____

_____

_____

_____

_____

_____

When you look at your questions above, describe how you feel. Write what's happening inside you, as best you can.

_____

_____

_____

_____

_____

_____

_____

_____

Writing Prompts:

Use these prompts to process the why question further. Try not to edit in your mind as you go. Write freely.

"My biggest why question seems to be..." (after writing that question, continue to express where your heart and soul go next).

_____
_____
_____
_____
_____

"With regard to my biggest why question, I think it might help if I..."

_____
_____
_____
_____
_____
_____
_____

Poetry Writing Exercise:

Using the following list of words to spur you on, try writing a poem that expresses some of your "Why?" questions. Don't worry about rhyme or composition. Express your heart and soul.

Heart   Soul   Why   Questions   Pain
Grief   Heal   Afraid   Remember

_____

_____

_____

_____

_____

_____

_____

_____

_____

_____

_____

_____

"Why?" is a natural and common question for a grieving heart. Keep expressing your why questions as they come. Get them out. Process them as best you can. Be patient with yourself. Accept yourself as you are in the moment, as best you can.

25

ANGER WITH GOD

In the grief process, many find themselves angry with God at some point.

Experiencing some anger is natural and common for a grieving heart. Anger looks for a target. We naturally search for who or what is responsible for our loved one's death. We have various targets available.

We might blame family members or friends that caused our loved one stress. Perhaps we hold past abusers, medical professionals, or people around our loved one when they died as responsible. Our anger might become focused on things or situations like cancer, heart disease, a flawed medical system, a stressful job, poor safety protocols, natural disasters, or war.

Once the blame begins, many of us eventually turn to God. After all, we reason, the buck stops with Him. "Why did God allow this?" "Why didn't He do something to stop this?" "Did God do this? Why?" "Why did God take them from me?"

Whatever our questions, our souls need to express them outwardly. We need to "get the questions out," as many times as necessary. If we're angry at God, we need to find healthy ways to express it.

"But it's not okay to be angry with God!" some might say. Even if we think this, however, it doesn't change the fact that we are angry with Him. And if He is God, He knows this already. We can't hide from Him or from ourselves. Good relationships thrive on trust. Part of trust is being willing and able to share what's happening inside us with the other party.

Even if you don't believe in God, you can still find yourself angry with Him. This is not unusual. Like other grief emotions, "getting it out" is key to the healing process.

When you think about your loss, what questions do you have for God? List them here.

_____

_____

_____

_____

_____

_____

_____

If you've been upset or angry with God since your loss, begin to write about this below. Write whatever comes to mind.

_____

_____

_____

_____

_____

_____

_____

_____

Letter Writing Exercise

Write a letter to God expressing what you're thinking and feeling about Him and your loss. Tell Him what you're angry about. Express your angst and frustration to Him. Get it out.

_____

_____

_____

_____

_____

_____

_____

_____

_____

_____

_____

_____

_____

_____

_____

_____

_____

_____

Being angry with God at some point in the grief process is common. Don't keep this inside. Get it out. Get the anger out in healthy ways. If He is God, He already knows. He can handle your anger.

26

SPIRITUAL / FAITH RELATIONSHIPS

We expect people of similar faith to be compassionate and supportive. Most of them are, at least for a little while. Some, however, will probably disappoint us.

They will say unhelpful things. They might spout spiritual platitudes and clichés at us rather than listening. They might not know how to be supportive, so they distance themselves and pull away from us. Perhaps they even ignore us altogether. Maybe they try to fix us and our loss somehow.

When these things happen, we naturally feel misunderstood, belittled, or even rejected.

People don't deal well with pain and grief, even people of faith. Most people tend to run when they feel uncomfortable. They feel insecure and out-of-control. Perhaps our grief triggers theirs, and they simply don't want to go into the pain again.

Whatever the reason, lack of support from people of like faith can be confusing, frustrating, and angering. Processing these disappointments will be crucial for our hearts and souls.

Have people of like faith disappointed you in your grief process? Describe some of this.

___

___

___

___

___

___

___

___

Specifically, what have people said and done that has shocked, confused, or frustrated you?

___

___

___

___

___

___

___

___

Letter Writing Exercise

Write a letter to those of similar faith who have disappointed you since your loss. Tell them how you feel about what they said and did. Tell them what you wish they had done or said instead. Don't overthink this. Write whatever comes to mind.

After a loss, there's no guarantee that those of like faith will understand or be supportive. Lowering our expectations and processing painful interactions are important.

27

SPIRITUAL DOUBTS AND FAITH CRISES

Loss can shake our souls. What we believe can come under some intense examination. Perhaps we now doubt some things we were sure of. Maybe we become sure of some things that we doubted. Most of us wonder about how all this fits together.

Spiritual questioning is common in the grief process. Doubts about various things surface in many grieving hearts. Being honest with ourselves and letting our hearts express these things is key to our future healing and growth.

We can begin to process questions and doubts by acknowledging and identifying them. Once identified, we can talk and write about them. Again, as with all aspects of grief, expressing what's happening inside us is crucial.

Heavy loss can lead some into a faith crisis (or crises) where most of what they believed before is called into question. Acknowledging and processing this is essential, though it might be scary. Some of the best things in life can be unnerving and hard.

Are there things that you believed before your loss that you now doubt or wonder about? List those things here.

_____

_____

_____

_____

_____

_____

_____

_____

Is there someone you consider to be a spiritual mentor of sorts? Do you sense you could share with them some of what's happening inside you? What do you think might be the benefit of this?

_____

_____

_____

_____

_____

_____

_____

_____

Writing Prompts:

Use the following prompts to dig deeper into this topic. Write freely. Try not to censor yourself. Get it out.

"The thoughts and doubts that are the most disturbing to me are..."

___

"When I think about these questions and doubts, I'm afraid that..."

Memory Writing Exercise:

When you think about some of the questions and doubts you have, what memories of your loved one come to mind?

_____

_____

_____

_____

_____

_____

_____

_____

_____

Pick one of these memories and write about it below. Let your heart express itself.

_____

_____

_____

_____

As with other parts of the grief process, please don't attempt to do this alone. Connect with someone you trust who will listen well and walk with you in this.

Try not to look too far down the road. Stay in the now as much as possible by being honest about and processing what is. As you do this, your next steps will become clearer with time.

28

SPIRITUAL FATIGUE AND NUMBNESS

Loss and the resulting grief can be exhausting emotionally, physically, and spiritually. Even our souls can become weary.

When we are spiritually fatigued, we can become numb. We zone out spiritually. We can feel empty, listless, and even lifeless.

Spiritual numbness can be disturbing. It feels like we've entered an unknown wilderness. We're trying to trudge forward, but every step seems to take massive energy and effort. The color of life has been muted. Everything seems dull and drab.

Reminding ourselves that now is not forever is important. Things will change. As we accept ourselves where we are and process our grief well, we will heal over time.

Connecting with a trusted spiritual mentor can be encouraging and help give us perspective. We all need safe people we respect who we can share with and listen to. If we don't have such a person in our lives, we might ask ourselves who might fill this role.

Many grieving hearts experience spiritual fatigue and numbness. This is common and natural. Acknowledging what's happening and "getting it out" can be helpful and relieving.

Are you experiencing some spiritual fatigue or numbness in your grief journey? (Or have you in the past?) Describe what this is like.

_____
_____
_____
_____
_____
_____
_____
_____

When you are spiritually exhausted or numb, how do you feel about yourself?

_____
_____
_____
_____
_____
_____
_____
_____

Writing Prompts:

Use these prompts to explore this more. As you write, let your heart go where it wants to. Record whatever comes to mind.

"When I think of myself spiritually, I'm most concerned that..."

_____

_____

_____

_____

_____

_____

_____

"When it comes to feeling spiritually exhausted and numb, I hope that..."

_____

_____

_____

_____

_____

_____

_____

Poetry Writing Exercise:

Think about spiritual fatigue and numbness for a moment. What words come to mind? Make a list of these words here:

_____

_____

_____

_____

Using the above words, write a brief poem. Don't worry about rhyme, meter, or format. Don't overthink it. Write.

_____

_____

_____

_____

_____

_____

_____

_____

Spirituality and faith run deep and tend to be emotionally charged. Feeling empty or numb spiritually can be disconcerting and even frightening. Take your heart and soul seriously. Process what's happening inside you.

29

SPIRITUAL GROWTH

Many grieving hearts report that times of loss can be times of great spiritual growth. Loss and grief can teach us many lessons. Some of these lessons are life-changing and deeply spiritual in nature.

We all want to live from our hearts. We want to love and be loved. We want to live with meaning and purpose. We want our days to count toward something greater than ourselves.

Loss teaches us that almost anything can happen to anyone at any time. On the one hand, that can be terrifying. It can also be incredibly freeing. We discover what really matters to us. We can begin to live more in the moment and focus on taking one step at a time.

Loss can lead us to look deeply into our own hearts and souls. If we're willing, we can honor those we've lost by living with more meaning and purpose than ever before.

Much of life is about overcoming. Spiritual growth is possible during times of deep emotional pain and traumatic loss. This can be part of our healing process.

When you think about spiritual growth, what kind of things come to mind? What does spiritual growth look like to you?

_____

_____

_____

_____

_____

_____

How would you describe where you are spiritually at present?

_____

_____

_____

_____

_____

_____

Below is a portion of the Serenity Prayer by Reinhold Niebuhr. Read through it several times.

> "God, grant me the grace to accept with serenity the things that cannot be changed,
> The courage to change the things that should be changed,
> And the wisdom to distinguish the one from the other.
> Living one day at time,
> Enjoying one moment at a time,
> Accepting hardship as a pathway to peace."

What strikes you about this portion of Niebuhr's prayer? Write and express what happens inside you as you read it.

_____

_____

_____

_____

_____

_____

_____

_____

_____

Write your own prayer. Try not to overthink this. Focus on honestly expressing your heart. Even if you don't believe in God, try this and see where it takes you.

_____

_____

_____

_____

_____

_____

_____

_____

_____

_____

_____

Spirituality can be a huge part of life. Many grieving hearts experience great spiritual growth during their seasons of loss. As you process your grief well, spiritual growth is surely possible for you as well.

In case you're interested, here is the entire Serenity Prayer.

> "God, grant me the grace to accept with serenity
> the things that cannot be changed,
>
> The courage to change the things that should be changed,
>
> And the wisdom to distinguish the one from the other.
>
> Living one day at time,
>
> Enjoying one moment at a time,
>
> Accepting hardship as a pathway to peace.
>
> Taking, as Jesus did, this sinful world as it is
>
> And not as I would have it,
>
> Trusting that You will make all things right
>
> As I surrender to Your will,
>
> That I might be reasonably happy with You in this life
>
> And supremely happy with You forever in the next.
>
> Amen."

PART FIVE:

MANAGING RELATIONSHIPS

When a close loss occurs, massive change begins
to trickle down into every corner of our lives.

Eventually, if not immediately, we sense the tremors starting to
shake our relationships with family, friends, and coworkers.

People treat us differently. Some people we counted on disappear.
Others are critical and judgmental. Still others obviously want to
support us but don't know how. New people show up in our lives.

The relational turnover can be staggering. In this section,
we'll begin to process some of the relational upheaval
that commonly follows the loss of someone special.

For many grieving hearts, this is the most painful
area of their grief journey. Breathe deeply. Take
your time. Use extra pages if you need to.

30

CHANGING RELATIONSHIPS

Loss is an unasked for, unsought, and unwanted force that impacts every area of our lives and brings stressful changes. Loss naturally changes us. We're not the same people we were before. As a result, loss also automatically hits all our relationships.

People respond to loss and grief differently. The people around us become aware of what has happened and begin to respond to it in their own ways. We have no say or control over this.

As a general rule, people don't respond well to loss, emotional pain, and grief. We tend to flee from such things rather than embracing them. Many grieving hearts begin to experience this on some level from their coworkers, friends, and even family.

Change is a constant in our lives. A loss brings change we were not expecting and could not possibly fully prepare ourselves for. Almost all of our relationships are jostled in some ways.

Have you sensed some relational shifts since your loss? Describe them.

_____
_____
_____
_____
_____
_____

Do you sense people are looking at you differently now? How so?

_____
_____
_____
_____
_____
_____
_____
_____
_____

Writing Prompts:

Use these prompts to express your heart about some of what's happening in your circle of relationships.

"Since my loss, I've noticed that people..."

_____

_____

_____

_____

_____

_____

_____

"When people see me or hear about my loss, I wish that they would..."

_____

_____

_____

_____

_____

_____

_____

Loss typically brings great relational changes in its wake. Many grieving hearts experience upheaval in even their closest relationships. Processing theses upsets and expressing what's happening inside you are crucial.

31

FIVE PEOPLE WE MEET IN GRIEF

The people we encounter will respond differently to us during a time of loss. We will meet different kinds of people on our grief journey.

Most people will mean well, but what they say and do is unhelpful. They don't know what to say, so they say what they've heard others say. They don't know what to do, so they tend to do nothing.

Some people are fixers. They try to help us feel better. They give advice we haven't asked for. They say and do things that tend to belittle our grief by trying to slap tiny Band-Aids on our gaping wounds. They try to fix the unfixable.

Others are critical judges. They evaluate how they think you're doing and let you know that your behavior is unacceptable. They shake their heads in disgust. They tell us to move on and to get over it.

Some are safe people. They meet us in our grief and accept us as we are. They listen. Their only agenda is to lovingly support us by walking with us as best they can.

Then there are fellow grievers. They too are in a season of loss. They can see our pain and relate. They can go beyond sympathy to empathy. Yet, fellow grievers can be any of the people above. They can be well-meaning but unhelpful. They can be fixers or even judges. They can be safe, supportive people.

You will encounter these five people on your grief journey. How you respond to them in your heart matters.

Think of these five people: the well-meaning but unhelpful person, the fixer, the critical judge, the safe person, and the fellow griever. Have you met all these people since your loss? Try to give an example of each one.

_____

_____

_____

_____

_____

_____

_____

Of these five people, which one tends to frustrate you the most? Describe why.

_____

_____

_____

_____

_____

_____

_____

_____

Writing Prompts:

Use the following prompts to dig deeper into your thoughts and feelings about these five people.

"As I think of the five people I will meet on my grief journey, what comes to mind is..."

___

___

___

___

___

___

___

___

___

___

"What frustrates me most about how people seem to be responding to me is..."

___

___

___

The people around you will respond differently to you during this time. Chances are, this will alter some of your relationships. You are not in control of others' responses. Focus on expressing what's happening inside you as honestly and thoroughly as possible.

Memory Writing Exercise:

When you think of the five types of people in this chapter, what memories of your interactions come to mind? Think about your interactions with others since your loss.

_____

_____

_____

_____

_____

_____

_____

Write about the memory above that disturbs you the most. Describe what happened and how you felt. Get it out.

_____

_____

_____

_____

_____

_____

_____

_____

_____

32

DISAPPEARING PEOPLE

After a loss, some people seem to disappear on us. One minute they're there expressing sympathy and the next, poof, they're gone.

We count on certain people for support during our grief. We naturally look to our friends, family, and perhaps some others for understanding and comfort. Sadly, some of these people will most likely distance themselves from us in some way. They might say, "We're here for you," but then we never see or hear from them.

These disappearances are common on the grief journey. Loss and grief are hard and uncomfortable. Many don't want to even be around emotional pain in any way. Perhaps our grief reminds them of their losses and triggers pain buried in their hearts.

For whatever reason, they don't show up. They were there before, but now they're gone. This can be incredibly painful. We were already hurting enough, but this relational distancing adds salt to our wounds.

Grief is never about just one loss. One loss brings change that automatically spawns other losses.

Have you experienced people distancing themselves from you since your loss? Describe this and how you feel about it.

_____

_____

_____

_____

_____

_____

Why do you think some people have chosen not to show up in your life during this time?

_____

_____

_____

_____

_____

_____

_____

_____

Letter Writing Exercise

Write a letter to those who have disappeared or distanced themselves from you since your loss. This is, of course, a letter you will never send. Be honest. Express how you feel. Get it out.

_____
_____
_____
_____
_____
_____
_____
_____
_____
_____
_____
_____
_____
_____
_____
_____

Having people we counted on disappear on us is a common experience on the grief journey. Expressing how you feel about this is important. Don't let the angst and frustration bury itself in your heart. Process these disappearances as best you can, as often as you need to.

33

UNSUPPORTIVE PEOPLE

It would be nice if everyone we knew and encountered was compassionate and supportive. Unfortunately, this is not the case.

Most people will not understand. Many will not want anything to do with us while we're grieving. Some will be supportive, but others will not.

We're naturally disappointed and hurt by this. Our broken hearts can be further wounded by both people who are close to us and by strangers and those we barely know.

At a time when we desperately need care and support, unsupportive people and their responses to us can add to our pain and sense of loss.

Over 3000 years ago, wise King Solomon said, "Above all else, guard your heart, for it is the spring from which everything else in your life flows." Since we can't control how other people react and respond to us and our grief, we must take steps to guard our own hearts. More on this later.

Have you encountered some unsupportive people in your grief process? List some of the unsupportive comments, body language, and actions that have come at you so far.

_____

_____

_____

_____

_____

_____

When others are unsupportive, how have you responded?

_____

_____

_____

_____

_____

_____

_____

_____

_____

Writing Prompts:

Think of one particular instance where someone was not supportive, and you walked away hurt and wounded. Use the following prompts to process this event.

"When this happened, I felt..."

_____
_____
_____
_____
_____
_____
_____

"What I wish that person could understand is that..."

_____
_____
_____
_____
_____
_____
_____
_____

Poetry Writing Exercise:

Using the following list of words, try writing a poem about your interactions with those who have been less than supportive since your loss. Let it rip. Express your mind and heart.

Heart   Broken   Pain   Wounded   Shocked
Wish   Angry   Words

_____

_____

_____

_____

_____

_____

_____

_____

_____

_____

_____

_____

Sadly, encountering unsupportive people is common for grieving hearts. Since this is inevitable, we need to find ways to guard our hearts during this time. We can begin to do that by processing these new wounds. We need to "get it out" so that we can begin to release these things and be less affected by them.

34

EXPECTATIONS

We all have expectations.

We have expectations of ourselves, of others, and of the world around us. Others have expectations of us - what we will do and say and how we will behave.

Expectations can be sneaky. We're unaware of many of them. Most expectations go unnoticed and unspoken. As a result, an expectation is often an invitation to disappointment.

We have expectations of the grief process and how it is going to go. We have expectations of ourselves and how we will handle all this. We have expectations of how others should respond to us. When these expectations aren't met and things don't go the way we anticipated, our angst, frustration, confusion, anxiety, fear, and depression are intensified.

We can guard our hearts a little better by identifying and evaluating our expectations of ourselves and others.

How did you anticipate your grief process would go? List some of the expectations you had.

_____
_____
_____
_____
_____
_____
_____

Think of a time when a particular expectation you had (of yourself or of others) was not met and you were hurt or disappointed. Describe what that was like for you.

_____
_____
_____
_____
_____
_____
_____
_____

Writing Prompts:

Use the following prompts to identify and process some of the expectations you have of yourself and others. Write freely whatever comes to mind. Try not to overthink or analyze. Focus on "getting it out."

"Some expectations I have of myself right now are..."

_____

_____

_____

_____

_____

_____

"Some expectations I have of others are..."

_____

_____

_____

_____

_____

_____

_____

_____

Take a few moments and read what you've written. Are these expectations realistic at present? If not, consider how you might release yourself and others from these burdens.

Memory Writing Exercise:

Think of a time since your loss when your expectations weren't met. Let the events and interactions around that disappointment surface in your mind.

Write about this memory below. Be as thorough and specific as you can. Express how you felt and what you thought.

_____

_____

_____

_____

_____

_____

_____

_____

Having expectations is natural. The grief journey is already challenging enough without carrying the excess burden of unrealistic expectations. When you find yourself frustrated, angry, or disappointed, ask yourself, "What expectation did I have that was not met?"

_____

_____

_____

Identifying and releasing our expectations is one way we can guard our hearts. This helps us process our grief in healthy ways.

35

SAFE PEOPLE

We all need safe people in our lives, especially when we're grieving.

Safe people don't evaluate or judge us. They don't give advice we haven't asked for. They don't try to fix the unfixable. They aren't threatened by our grief. They don't make it about themselves.

Safe people meet us where we are and accept us as we are. They are great listeners. They enter our world and exist with us there. They have no agenda other than to support us by being with us in our pain.

Our hearts sense when we're in the presence of a safe person. We begin to relax a little bit. Just seeing them or hearing their voice can bring relief.

Safe people are key players on our grief journey. They are excellent traveling companions as we traverse this dark, often scary wilderness.

If we don't have any safe people in our lives, we need to find some. They're out there - ready and willing to support us.

Do you have safe people in your life? List their names. Next to each name, describe why they are a safe person to you.

_____

_____

_____

_____

_____

_____

If you don't have safe people in your life, or you need a few more, where do you think you might find them? Brainstorm some options.

_____

_____

_____

_____

_____

_____

_____

_____

_____

Writing Prompts:

Use these prompts to further process this concept of safe people and the role they can play in your life.

"When I think of the safe people in my life, I'm thankful that they..."

_____

_____

_____

_____

_____

Imagine yourself to be a safe person who wants to support other grieving hearts. "As a safe person, I can care for and support others by..."

_____

_____

_____

_____

_____

Safe people aren't perfect. They make mistakes. On the whole, however, they are kind, compassionate, loving, and supportive. They are priceless jewels in this wasteland of grief.

Connect often with your safe people. Your heart needs this.

36

WORK RELATIONSHIPS

Work relationships can be challenging, even when life is fairly smooth and steady. When we're grieving, the degree of difficulty at work tends to go way up.

Fundamentally, work is about performance. We meet the requirements of our job and hopefully even exceed them. We strive to meet the expectations placed upon us. We want to do well.

When loss strikes, grief begins to gobble up our mental and emotional energy. As grief takes up more and more space in our lives, there's less of us available for our work. Our performance is naturally affected. Work can provide some much-needed distraction from our grief, but the additional weight we now carry can weigh us down. We're already exhausted and work requires more energy that we don't have.

Our coworkers might be compassionate, for a while. Our bosses, supervisors, and colleagues will expect us to "return to normal" and work efficiently and effectively as soon as possible. Even though our lives have changed, it's still business as usual for them.

Navigating and managing our work relationships adds an extra layer of challenge to our already taxed hearts, minds, and bodies.

Have you noticed a change in your work performance since your loss? How so?

How have your boss, supervisor, and coworkers responded to your loss so far?

Writing Prompts:

Use the following prompts to process what's happening at work. Write freely. Jot down whatever comes to mind. Let your heart express itself.

"When I'm at work, I find myself wondering..."

_____

_____

_____

_____

_____

_____

"My coworkers could support me best right now by..."

_____

_____

_____

_____

_____

_____

_____

Letter Writing Exercise

Write a letter to your boss, supervisor, and work colleagues. What would you like to be able to say to them about your loss and what you're experiencing right now? Include how they might support and care for you during this time.

_____
_____
_____
_____
_____
_____
_____
_____
_____
_____
_____
_____
_____
_____
_____
_____
_____

Work relationships can be difficult, especially when we're tired and grieving. If it's possible, consider checking in with your boss or supervisor and share with them how you're doing. You might want to share the content of the letter you wrote. If they ask how they can support you, tell them.

These conversations can be frightening, but they can also be good and healing. Of course, not every boss or supervisor is even open to such a conversation. Listen to your heart. Be wise. Consult someone safe and trustworthy for their input. Be kind to yourself.

37

SPOUSE AND PARTNER RELATIONSHIPS

Loss can be hard on marriages and partner relationships. Even if we're both experiencing the same loss (a child, a common friend, a beloved parent or in-law, etc.), we will certainly grieve differently.

After a close loss, some don't feel supported by their spouses or partners. Instead of compassion and patience, they sense pressure to "get over it" and "move on." They want us "back to normal" and for life to go back to the way it was.

Others feel supported and loved by their life partners but sense a new distance creeping into their relationship. We're changing and perhaps they don't know what to do with that.

Loss hits our most significant relationships too. As we grieve, it will affect our marriage or partner relationship. Our world has been turned upside down and all of our relationships are being jostled.

These relational changes can be unnerving and disconcerting. Navigating these changes well is a key part of the grief journey.

Since your loss, have you noticed changes in your relationship with your spouse or partner? If so, describe these changes.

_____
_____
_____
_____
_____
_____
_____

In your marriage relationship, what are you concerned about at present?

_____
_____
_____
_____
_____
_____
_____
_____

Writing Prompts:

Use these prompts to dig a little deeper into this subject. Be honest. Write freely. Resist the temptation to edit or censor yourself. "Get it out."

"I wonder what my spouse is thinking about…"

___

"I wish that my partner…"

___

Letter Writing Exercise

Write a letter to your spouse or partner about how you would like them to support you during this time. What do you want them to know about you and your grief? What would be most helpful to you? What do you want and need from them right now?

Consider sharing these things with them. Ask them if they are willing to just listen. Conversations like these can be scary, but they can also be incredibly positive and healing.

A marriage or life partnership takes two to succeed. You have no control over your partner and how they respond. All you can do is love them as best you can and share what you can as you walk this grief road.

38

PARENTING IN GRIEF

"There is a sacredness in tears. They are not the mark of weakness, but of power. They speak more eloquently than ten thousand tongues. They are the messengers of overwhelming grief, of deep contrition, and of unspeakable love."

- Washington Irving

Parenting is tough. In fact, it may be one of life's toughest tasks.

In essence, parenting is not so much a task as an ongoing, dynamic relationship. Good parenting, like a good marriage, is a moving target. Things are always changing.

Parenting while grieving presents some unique challenges. If our kids are still at home, we're still responsible for providing, protecting, and leading them amid all the upheaval of this loss. Our desire to "be strong" for them can lead us to stuff our grief and put on a good front. Though this sounds good, it's usually not healthy for us, and it doesn't teach our kids how to handle loss and grieve well (a skill that they will desperately need in life).

If our children are adults, chances are they will respond in various ways to us as a grieving parent. Many will try to protect us and fix our grief. Some will get irritated and send signals to us saying, "Get over it and feel better already." Some might be compassionate, supportive, and understanding.

In any case, our job is to live from our hearts. That means expressing our grief and what's happening inside us in healthy ways. That includes being honest and open about our grief with our children, according to their age and ability to understand. It's okay and healthy for them to see us express our emotions. By sharing our grief with them, we're modeling some key life skills for them.

Our children will face loss. They already have. We have an opportunity to teach and lead them by how we respond to our loss. This might be uncomfortable or embarrassing for us. That's okay. Grieving in healthy ways in front of our kids is part of loving them well.

How do you sense your children are responding to your grief so far?

_____

_____

_____

_____

_____

_____

What do you wish you could say to your kids about what's happening in your life?

_____

_____

_____

_____

_____

Writing Prompts:

Use the following prompts to write more about parenting during this challenging time.

"When I think about sharing some of my grief with my children, I wonder about..."

_____
_____
_____
_____
_____
_____
_____

"If I had to guess, I think my kids are looking at me and wondering..."

_____
_____
_____
_____
_____
_____
_____
_____

Memory Writing Exercise:

Think about your interactions with your children since your loss. What conversations and situations come to mind?

___

Pick one of these memories and write about it below. Describe what happened and what was said. Express what you thought and how you felt.

_____

_____

_____

_____

_____

_____

_____

_____

_____

_____

_____

_____

_____

_____

_____

If your children have experienced the same loss (a grandparent, a parent, a sibling, another family member or family friend), consider having a time together of sharing memories. If they are young, you could draw pictures for or about your loved one. Giving your family a chance to grieve together can be a good and precious gift.

39

FAMILY RELATIONSHIPS

Family can be wonderful. These relationships can also be stressful. When loss and grief get thrown into the mix, some family relationships can be tested.

Some families are incredibly supportive during crisis and loss. Other families are somewhat sympathetic but not helpful. Still others are critical and even toxic.

Most families, however, contain all three of the above. As we grieve, it becomes apparent who is safe and trustworthy right now and who is not.

As with all relationships, getting around people who are helpful to us and limiting our exposure to those who aren't is key. We can focus on expressing our grief in healthy ways to those who are open to listening and accepting us where we are.

Chances are, our family will surprise us during our grief journey. Some we thought would be compassionate and supportive may not be. Some we thought would be neutral might step up and become major players during this time.

Whatever the case, managing our family relationships well during this time can aid greatly in our healing process.

Since your loss, have you noticed any changes in your relationship with other family members? How so?

_____

_____

_____

_____

_____

_____

Looking back, how did you anticipate family members would respond to you and your grief?

_____

_____

_____

_____

_____

_____

_____

_____

_____

Writing Prompts:

Use these prompts to think and write more about your family's role in your grief process.

"When I think about my grief and my family, I am thankful for..."

_____

_____

_____

_____

_____

_____

"When it comes to family members' response to me and my grief, it would be helpful if..."

_____

_____

_____

_____

_____

_____

If you haven't already done so, consider approaching the family members you sense want to help and be supportive. Tell them a little about what your grief journey is like. Share with them what they can do that would be helpful to you.

Perhaps you're afraid of being disappointed. That's natural. After all, you're dealing with enough pain as it is. Yet taking a risk like this could be more than worth it. By sharing with trusted family members, you're inviting them into your grief world. That helps them too, more than you realize.

40

GUARDING YOUR HEART

Our hearts are our most valuable possession. They are the guts of who we are.

This world is not kind to hearts - especially grieving hearts. Life blazes forward with stunning speed. Often, we are dragged along with it, sometimes kicking and screaming. No one likes grief and pain. We avoid such things at all cost.

Grieving in healthy ways demands that we guard our hearts. We do that by expressing honestly what's happening inside us. We connect with people who are helpful to us and limit our exposure to those who aren't. We pursue practices and habits that lead to healing and overall wellness.

Making sure our hearts get the nurturing they need is a massive part of our recovery and healing. At a time when our tank is nearly always empty, we need good, healthy inflow. We welcome messages and influences that are truthful, loving, and compassionate. We begin to weed out information and influences that are upsetting, confusing, and toxic to our grief process.

We need to guard our "eye gate" and our "ear gate." We can't unsee or unhear something. We're profoundly impacted by what we take in. This is a time when we need to be vigilant about what we choose to expose ourselves to.

What do we need in our lives right now? Comfort? Acceptance? Love? Peace? Calm? Hope? Meaning?

Whatever we need, that is what we need to seek. What kind of information, people, and influences are healthy for us and can meet our needs?

Limiting negative influences is important. Seeking positive and healing inflow into our lives is also key to the healing process.

When you hear the phrase, "Guard your heart," what comes to mind?

___

___

___

___

___

___

___

What are some influences (and people) that you know are not healthy for you right now?

___

___

___

___

___

___

___

___

Writing Prompts:

Use these prompts to delve more into what it might mean to guard your heart during this season of grief.

"When I think of things or people who might nurture me and help heal my wounded heart, I think of..."

_____

_____

_____

_____

_____

_____

_____

"When it comes to guarding my eye gate and ear gate, I think I need to..."

_____

_____

_____

_____

_____

_____

_____

Poetry Writing Exercise:

Using the following list of words, try writing a poem about guarding your heart. Feel free to use any other words you wish in addition to these. Don't overthink it. Don't worry about rhyme, meter, or composition. Free your heart to use these words to express what you think and feel.

Heart   Soul   Guard   Protect   Nurture
Heal   Wound   Pain   Grief   Afraid

_____
_____
_____
_____
_____
_____
_____
_____
_____
_____
_____
_____

The world is often not kind to grieving hearts. Your heart is the core of who you are. Guard it well. Nurture it. You're more important than you realize.

PART SIX:

MANAGING THE FUTURE

When we experience a heavy loss, the
future we anticipated changed.

We don't realize this at first. With each passing day, however, we become increasingly aware of the domino effect this loss has had on our hopes, dreams, and expectations.

If the loss is close enough, most of our future might appear dark and hazy. We wonder what's out there for us. What will we do? What will life be like? Who will we be now?

In this section, we'll begin to dig into how this loss has impacted your future. As you move through these pages, practice breathing deeply from time to time. You may discover things you had not thought of or realized before.

Be honest. Use extra pages as necessary. Focus on expressing your grief and "getting it out."

41

THE ANTICIPATED FUTURE

When loss comes to us, what we don't realize at the time is that our future has just been significantly altered. Depending on the closeness and severity of our loss, the future we anticipated may be gone.

We all have expectations. Most of these are subconscious, automatic, and unspoken. Though we might not have ever talked about them, we have many assumptions about the future. We count on certain things and people, without even realizing it.

When we lose a friend or loved one, we suddenly discover that the landscape ahead of us has changed. The world looks the same, but things are different now. Someone special is missing.

Part of the grief journey includes coming face-to-face with a future that is now different from what we anticipated. This can bring a profound sense of more loss. We not only mourn the loss of the person, but also of everything attached to them, including our future expectations.

Before your loss, what assumptions did you have about the future? Make a list of the things you anticipated that included your friend or loved one.

_____
_____
_____
_____
_____
_____

Out of your list above, choose three of the most painful losses. Write these lost expectations down again here. Beside each one, express a little about how you feel about that loss.

_____
_____
_____
_____
_____
_____
_____
_____

Writing Prompts:

Use the following prompts to process more about the future you anticipated. Try not to edit as you write. Express your thoughts freely.

"When I look at the future now, I wonder..."

_____
_____
_____
_____
_____
_____
_____
_____
_____

"Some of the expectations I have now about the future are..."

_____
_____
_____
_____
_____

The reality is that each day is new. Every moment is uncharted territory. We have never been at this particular time and place before. Change is one thing we can always count on. Part of grieving well includes learning to hold all things loosely and to live in the present as much as possible. Expressing our grief about the loss of what we expected is important.

42

LOST HOPES AND DREAMS

As we said in the last chapter, when we lose someone, we also lose much of what was attached to them. Most likely, this includes some of our hopes and dreams.

At best, our future hopes that included the one we lost are now significantly altered. At worst, these hopes are shattered, crushed, and gone.

Our future hopes and dreams might have included certain relationships, places, houses, and financial circumstances. Perhaps certain scenarios about what we would do, where we would go, and what we would experience were in the mix.

The one we lost will not come home again. They will no longer go to work. They will not come around the corner. They will not attend future births, graduations, weddings, or other special events. Every mental image we have of the future that included them has now been altered or has completely disappeared.

When we lose someone special, we not only grieve what we lost, but also what will now never be in this life. This can be incredibly painful and disorienting. Being kind to ourselves in this process is crucial.

What are some of things you hoped for in the future that have now changed? Make a list of them here.

_____

_____

_____

_____

_____

_____

From the list above, which lost hope or dream is the most painful for you right now? Describe this loss and the pain you feel about it.

_____

_____

_____

_____

_____

_____

_____

_____

_____

Letter Writing Exercise

Write a letter to the loved one or friend that is no longer here. Tell them what you're going to miss about the future. Share with them the hopes and dreams that you had. Express your heart to them, as honestly as you can.

_____

_____

_____

_____

_____

_____

_____

_____

_____

_____

_____

_____

_____

_____

_____

_____

_____

_____

Acknowledging and identifying lost hopes and dreams is an important part of the grief journey. Expressing our thoughts and feelings about these future losses is part of taking care of ourselves and honoring our friend or loved one.

Breathe deeply. This journey is a one step, one moment at a time process.

43

FUTURE GRIEF BURSTS

"How lucky I am to have something that makes saying goodbye so hard."

- Winnie the Pooh (A. A. Milne)

There are times in the grief process where we sense we're healing. We believe we're doing better. Then we experience another grief attack. The emotions overwhelm us, and we feel like we're right back where we started. It can seem like the loss is happening all over again.

Sudden grief bursts months and even years after a loss are natural and common. We're minding our own business and out of the blue a grief lightning bolt strikes. Many times we can identify a trigger of some sort - a person, voice, place, aroma, song, etc. Other times, it feels like we got hit by the grief bus from behind without warning.

Grief bursts can be good and healing. The grief is within us and needs to be expressed. These sudden floods of emotion provide a pressure release for our hearts. The spillways of our grief reservoir open and what's inside comes cascading out.

One thing that can help is to proactively prepare for these surges in grief emotion. We can develop some exit strategies.

Option A might be to simply leave where we are and go to a private place (a restroom, our car, etc.). Then we breathe deeply and decide what we want to do. Option B might be to stay where we are, breathe deeply, and see if we can continue being where we are and doing what we're doing. Being proactive and giving ourselves a couple of options can be vastly relieving and helpful when grief bursts come.

We let the grief come. We feel it through. We process it as best we can. We're not going backwards. Grief bursts are unpredictable in the sense that they can happen anytime, anywhere, but they are natural and common.

Describe what a grief burst is like for you. Describe your feelings and thoughts during that time.

_____
_____
_____
_____
_____
_____
_____
_____
_____
_____
_____
_____
_____
_____
_____
_____

What do you think about Option A and B above as proactive possibilities for when grief bursts strike? Can you think of any more options? Try picturing yourself in a public place and having a grief burst. See yourself applying your options.

_____
_____
_____
_____
_____
_____
_____
_____
_____
_____
_____
_____
_____
_____
_____
_____
_____
_____
_____

Writing Prompts:

Use the following prompts to write more about grief bursts and how you would like to handle them.

"When I have a grief burst, I get concerned about..."

_____
_____
_____
_____
_____
_____
_____
_____
_____
_____
_____
_____
_____
_____
_____

"When a grief burst comes, I would like to be able to..."

___

Grief bursts are common and natural. They can be triggered by anything at any time. When they come, find time to process them, if you can.

Please don't view grief bursts as steps back. Your heart is expressing itself. Give your heart space to do so. Accept yourself as best you can in the moment.

44

HOLIDAYS AND SPECIAL TIMES

"What is there to do when people die, people so dear and rare, but bring them back by remembering."

-May Sarton

Special days fill our calendars. Birthdays. Anniversaries. Christmas. Thanksgiving. Holidays. Though these days are normally a day of joy, for those who are grieving these times can be extremely difficult.

Holidays and special days can surface our losses like nothing else. As these days approach, we're hyperaware of who's missing. When the special day comes, we bump into a memory with every step.

Navigating these times can be exhausting and challenging. The dread of these days alone can suck us dry and immobilize us.

As with the rest of the grief process, we need to find ways to process these times. The good news is that instead of hiding and hoping for the best (which never works well), we can resolve to meet these days with courage and use them to honor our loved one and to express our grief in meaningful ways.

The most important thing is to be proactive and make a simple plan for the day to remember those we've lost and to honor them.

In your grief process so far, what special days have been difficult for you? Describe what those days were like.

_____

_____

_____

_____

_____

_____

_____

As you look ahead, what special days are lurking in front of you? Which ones are you most concerned about and why?

_____

_____

_____

_____

_____

_____

_____

_____

Writing Prompts:

Use these prompts to process more about upcoming special days and how you can meet them well.

"When I think of the special days ahead, some things I might do to remember and honor my loved one are..." (Brainstorm a list of possibilities).

_____
_____
_____
_____
_____
_____
_____
_____
_____
_____
_____
_____

"With regard to the next special day coming up, I'm concerned that..."

_____
_____
_____

Don't ignore upcoming holidays and special days. Guard your heart by being proactive and making a simple plan to take care of yourself and honor your loved one that day.

IDEAS FOR HOLIDAYS AND SPECIAL OCCASIONS

Instead of dreading special days – anniversaries, birthdays, and holidays – focus on being proactive about these times and using them for good.

Here are a few ideas to help you take care of yourself and honor your loved one on these difficult days:

- Light a candle in their honor.
- Make a donation in their name.
- Serve in a cause that they were passionate about.
- Write them a letter telling them how much you love them and what you're thankful for.
- Invite a few others who knew your loved one to participate in a time of memory sharing.
- Remember and honor them by giving gifts to others in their name on their birthday or death anniversary.
- Set up a scholarship fund in their name.
- Set up an empty chair in remembrance of them at family gatherings and other special occasions.
- Intentionally include them in gatherings on holidays by inviting everyone to share something about them.
- Have a birthday party for them and ask others to bring a card that reminds them of your loved one. Have those attending share a memory or story.
- Host a butterfly release on the anniversary of their death.

- Give some of their possessions to others as items of remembrance.
- Get creative. Think about your loved one. What do you think might bring a smile to their face?

Pay attention to your heart. Use these special days to help you adjust, recover, heal, and grow.

45

IDENTITY CRISIS

After a heavy, close loss, our sense of identity can be shaken. Some losses change so much that we can wonder who we are now and what we're supposed to do.

We have many roles in life: child, sibling, student, parent, relative, friend, caregiver, employee, boss, citizen, organization member, etc. When we lose someone special, inevitably at least one of these roles is greatly affected or perhaps even erased. Though we are not what we do, we naturally wed some of our more important roles with who we are.

Our sense of who we are is key to how we live life. We live out and daily express who we truly believe ourselves to be. Our sense of identity is a major driver of our thoughts, emotions, and purpose. Having something taken from us that shakes our basic sense of who we are can be frightening.

Having at least some bit of identity crisis during a season of loss is common for grieving hearts. Processing our loss' impact on who we perceive ourselves to be is important.

List some of the roles you have in life (child, sibling, student, parent, relative, friend, caregiver, employee, boss, citizen, organization member, etc.).

_____

_____

_____

_____

_____

_____

_____

Which of these roles has been affected by your loss? Describe some of the changes.

_____

_____

_____

_____

_____

_____

_____

_____

Writing Prompts:

Use the following prompts to write about how this loss has affected your sense of who you are.

"I'm not the same person I was before. For example, now..."

_____

_____

_____

_____

_____

_____

"If I had to answer the question, 'Who am I?', I would say..."

_____

_____

_____

_____

_____

_____

Loss shakes our lives. It alters our personal worlds. Our sense of who we are can be jostled and upended. All of this is incredibly stressful. Breathe deeply. Be kind to yourself. Focus on "getting the grief out" in healthy ways. Live life one step, one moment at a time.

46

DECISION-MAKING

Making decisions is normally stressful and challenging. While we're grieving, decision-making can seem frightening and even impossible.

After a loss, our lives are anything but business as usual. There is always more flux and change going on than we realize. It's as if our world is shifting. We tend to be out of balance in many ways. This is natural since our emotions and our routines are shaken and tossed about.

Simple wisdom tells us to let things settle before making any big, life-altering decisions. Many in the grief world say, "Avoid making any major decisions for six months to a year after a heavy loss." When time-sensitive, large decisions must be made, we need to make certain we don't make them alone. We need to involve other people we trust who have expertise and wisdom in those areas.

Many grieving hearts experience decision-making paralysis during their grief journey. Even the smallest decision - like what to have for dinner - can be overwhelming. Something tragic has happened. We're missing someone dear to us. This can naturally catapult us into being hyper-careful about everything. We don't want to make any mistakes. We can't handle any missteps or extra trouble right now.

Some grieving hearts, on the other hand, will make quick, impulsive decisions. Making decisions is one way we can take action and "do something" to try and quell the underlying terror of feeling out of control. These quick, impulsive actions rarely produce good results, especially if they are big, life-changing decisions.

In our world, we are used to everything being quick and convenient. The grief process is neither. Grief cannot be hurried or pushed. Feeling better and healing are not goals that can be controlled and achieved by a checklist of actions and activities. The grief journey is not a straight sprint down a minor stretch of the highway of life. It is more like a meandering marathon through a thick, overgrown forest.

Since your loss, what has decision-making been like for you? Describe this.

_____

_____

_____

_____

_____

_____

What decisions do you sense are looming in front of you? Make a list of them here (even "small" decisions can be stressful!).

_____

_____

_____

_____

_____

_____

_____

Letter Writing Exercise

Write a letter to yourself about decision-making. Detach and pretend that you are a trusted friend and wise mentor. What would you say to yourself about decision-making in the months ahead? Write freely. Resist the temptation to edit. Be honest.

Take your time. Let patience rule. Resist making the big decisions that don't absolutely have to be made. Don't be rushed or bullied by others in this process. Guard your heart. Focus on grieving in healthy ways.

47

MISSION AND PURPOSE

A close loss can upend our personal lives to the point where even our purpose can be called into question. We can wonder who we are and why we're here. We can find ourselves thinking, "What's the point anyway?" We might even doubt whether life has any meaning.

Wondering about our purpose and mission is natural and common for those on the grief journey. If we're willing, this loss can help us further clarify who we are and what life is all about. The grief journey can fine tune our personal missions and move us to live with more passion and purpose than ever before.

When we lack a strong sense of purpose, our hearts go into hiding. We become like a piece of wood thrown into a river with a swift current. We get swept along, bobbing here and there, getting slammed against the rocks along the way. We're alive and making good time, but we don't know where we're going.

The grief journey gives us a unique opportunity to reevaluate our lives, including our purpose and direction. Our hearts have been broken. Life is different now. This is a time of questioning and change. Rather than simply being swept along, we can pay attention to what our healing hearts are saying to us.

Whatever our mission and purpose might be, it will surely be deeply connected to three things: people, love, and service. We're designed for relationship. We're wired to love and be loved. We're all interdependent on each other. We're in this together.

Since your loss, have you wondered about your purpose and mission in life (who you are and why you're here)? How so?

_____

_____

_____

_____

_____

_____

At this point, what would you say is your purpose in life? Why are you here?

_____

_____

_____

_____

_____

_____

_____

_____

Writing Prompts:

Use the following prompts to process more about your mission in life and why you're here. Remember to write freely and try not to edit or censor yourself as you go.

"If I had to put it into words, I would say that the meaning of life is..."

_____

_____

_____

_____

_____

_____

"Here's how I can use this loss to help me live out my purpose and mission:"

_____

_____

_____

_____

_____

_____

Letter Writing Exercise

Write a letter from your loved one or friend to yourself about your mission in life. What would they say to you about your purpose in life and why you are here?

_____

_____

_____

_____

_____

_____

_____

_____

_____

_____

_____

_____

_____

_____

_____

_____

Without a clear sense of purpose, we wander. We end up chasing things that don't matter. We pile up regrets. We allow the world around us to set our agenda rather than our internal priorities and values. Loss can teach us to dig deeper and to pay more attention to our hearts.

Our hearts are who we are. Part of processing our grief in healthy ways is reevaluating who we really are and becoming even more clear about our mission and purpose.

48

USING OUR GRIEF FOR GOOD

"Those who have suffered understand suffering and therefore extend their hand."

- Patti Smith

Many grieving hearts report that the thing that helped most in their grief process was finding ways to use their pain for good.

Grief can be overwhelming. We need breaks. We need to get out of our own heads for a while. Noticing those around us and serving others can temporarily focus our attention elsewhere. We get the small grief breaks we need and accomplish something meaningful. Others benefit and we can see some of the fruit of our actions. Serving others brings perspective. When we give, we end up receiving. When we serve, we heal a little.

Connecting with others and serving gives purpose to our pain. We're reminded that we're in this together. We need each other badly.

Service exercises our broken hearts. Hearts need this kind of exercise to be healthy. In times of pain and loss, we need to find ways to live with purpose. Our personal mission will ultimately boil down to people, relationships, love, and service.

How can we begin to use our grief for good? Are there ways we can serve those around us - our family, neighbors, friends, and co-workers? Is there a cause or organization we might volunteer with? Can we support other grieving hearts somehow?

Though our tank is low to empty, we need to get creative and reach out in service. Rather than draining us further, this puts a little back into our tank.

How might you serve others during this time? Brainstorm a list of possibilities. Get creative. Think outside the box.

_____
_____
_____
_____
_____
_____

Of the things you listed above, which ones are the most attractive to you?

_____
_____
_____
_____
_____
_____
_____

Writing Prompts:

Use the following prompts to talk more about serving others during your time of grief.

"When I think about serving others right now, I feel..."

"When it comes to reaching out and serving others, I am willing to..."

_____
_____
_____
_____
_____
_____
_____
_____
_____
_____
_____
_____
_____
_____

Using our grief for good is a key part of the healing process. Serving others helps us process our own grief better. Loving those around us - perhaps just by noticing them and expressing care for them - can bring some much-needed perspective and comfort.

Serving, giving, and loving others has inherent benefits. When we serve while grieving, everyone wins.

CONCLUDING THOUGHTS

Loss is painful. The grief journey is challenging and exhausting. Processing the grief inside and "getting it out" is key to recovery, adjustment, healing, and growth.

In this workbook, you've moved through various aspects of the grief process. You've engaged your heart in expressing what's happening inside you. You've tackled difficult issues, circumstances, and relationships.

The grief work you've done matters. Your heart, mind, body, and soul have all benefitted. Your relationships will be enriched as well, if that isn't happening already! Every step toward healing is a step forward.

Be kind to yourself.

Be patient with yourself.

Keep writing.

Make writing a daily habit.

Keep expressing what's happening inside you. Keep giving your heart avenues to vent and share.

As you travel this grief road, accept yourself as you are in the moment.

Accept others as they are. Get around people who are helpful to you and limit your exposure to those who aren't.

Guard and nurture your heart.

As you grieve well, seek to love well. Let your compassion deepen.

Use your grief for good. Make serving others a habit.

Keep this workbook / journal handy. Refer to it as needed. Engage in the writing exercises again. You'll be encouraged by how you've healed and grown.

I'm honored to be with you on this journey. Please visit me at www.garyroe.com. Feel free to contact me and share. I'm here to help, if I can.

And remember: You're not alone, you're not crazy, and you will make it through this.

Warmly,

Gary

Don't forget to download your free eBook (PDF):

Grief: 9 Things I Wish I Had Known

https://www.garyroe.com/grief-9-things-i-wish-i-had-known-ebook/

AN INVITATION TO MAKE A DIFFERENCE

When we serve others who are hurting, our own hearts heal a little. Over time, the comfort and caring we share with those around us can add up, bringing relief and greater health to our own wounded souls.

In the latter portion of this journal and workbook, we began thinking about how to use our grief to make a difference in this world and in the lives of others. If this interests you, I would like to invite you to consider becoming a part of my Difference Maker Community.

As a group, we are focused on making a positive, healing impact in the lives of those around us – especially other grieving hearts.

For more information, please contact me at contact@garyroe.com. Simply say, "I would like to know more about the Difference Maker Community," and I will respond to you personally.

Together, I believe we can make a massive difference.

Warmly,

Gary

Help us reach more grieving hearts.

Share this link: https://www.garyroe.com/grieving-the-write-way-series

Together, we can make a difference.

ADDITIONAL GRIEF RESOURCES

THE COMFORT SERIES

www.garyroe.com/comfort-series

Comfort for Grieving Hearts: Hope and Encouragement in Times of Loss

Comfort for the Grieving Spouse's Heart: Hope and Healing After Losing Your Partner

Comfort for the Grieving Adult Child's Heart: Hope and Healing After Losing Your Parent

Comfort for the Grieving Parent's Heart: Hope and Healing After Losing Your Child

THE GOD AND GRIEF SERIES

www.garyroe.com/god-and-grief-series

Grief Walk: Experiencing God After the Loss of a Loved One

Widowed Walk: Experiencing God After the Loss of a Spouse

Orphaned Walk: Experiencing God After the Loss of a Parent

THE GOOD GRIEF SERIES

https://www.garyroe.com/good-grief-series/

The Grief Guidebook: Common Questions, Compassionate Answers, Practical Suggestions

www.garyroe.com/grief-guidebook

Aftermath: Picking Up the Pieces After a Suicide

www.garyroe.com/aftermath

Shattered: Surviving the Loss of a Child

www.garyroe.com/shattered

Teen Grief: Caring for the Grieving Teenage Heart

www.garyroe.com/teengrief

Please Be Patient, I'm Grieving: How to Care for and Support the Grieving Heart www.garyroe.com/please-be-patient

Heartbroken: Healing from the Loss of a Spouse

www.garyroe.com/heartbroken-2

Surviving the Holidays Without You: Navigating Loss During Special Seasons

www.garyroe.com/surviving-the-holidays

THE DIFFERENCE MAKER SERIES

www.garyroe.com/difference-maker

Difference Maker: Overcoming Adversity and Turning Pain into Purpose, Every Day (Adult & Teen Editions)

Living on the Edge: How to Fight and Win the Battle for Your Mind and Heart (Adult & Teen Editions)

FREE ON GARY'S WEBSITE

Grief: 9 Things I Wish I had Known

In this deeply personal and practical eBook, Gary shares nine key lessons from his own grief journeys. "This was so helpful! I saw myself on every page," said one reader. "I wish I had read this years ago," said another. Widely popular, this eBook has brought hope and comfort to thousands of grieving hearts.

Available at www.garyroe.com

The Good Grief Mini-Course

Full of personal stories, inspirational content, and practical assignments, this 8-session email series is designed to help readers understand grief and deal with its roller-coaster emotions. Thousands have been through this course, which is now being used in support groups as well.

Available at www.garyroe.com.

The Hole in My Heart: Tackling Grief's Tough Questions

This eBook tackles some of grief's big questions: "How did this happen?" "Why?" "Am I crazy?" "Am I normal?" "Will this get any easier?" plus others. Written in the first person, it engages and comforts the heart.

Available at www.garyroe.com.

I Miss You: A Holiday Survival Kit

Thousands have downloaded this brief, easy-to-read, and very personal e-book. I Miss You provides some basic, simple tools on how to use holiday and special times to grieve well and love those around you.

Available at www.garyroe.com.

A REQUEST FROM THE AUTHOR

Thank you for taking your heart seriously and working through the *Grieving the Write Way Journal and Workbook*. I hope you found some comfort, healing, and practical help in these pages.

I would love to hear what you thought of this book. Would you consider taking a moment and sending me a few sentences on how the *Grieving the Write Way Journal and Workbook* impacted you?

Send me your thoughts at contact@garyroe.com.

Your comments and feedback mean a lot to me and will assist me in producing more quality resources for grieving hearts.

Thank you.

Warmly,

Gary

Help us reach other grieving hearts.

Share this link:
https://www.garyroe.com/grieving-the-write-way-series

CARING FOR GRIEVING HEARTS

Visit Gary at www.garyroe.com and connect with him on Facebook, Twitter, LinkedIn, and Pinterest

Links:
Facebook: https://www.facebook.com/garyroeauthor
Twitter: https://twitter.com/GaryRoeAuthor
LinkedIn: https://www.linkedin.com/in/garyroeauthor
Pinterest: https://www.pinterest.com/garyroe79/

ABOUT THE AUTHOR

Gary's story began with a childhood of mixed messages and sexual abuse. This was followed by other losses and numerous grief experiences.

Ultimately, a painful past led Gary into a life of helping wounded people heal and grow. A former college minister, missionary in Japan, entrepreneur in Hawaii, pastor, and hospice chaplain, he now serves as a writer, speaker, grief specialist, and grief coach.

In addition to *Grieving the Write Way Journal and Workbook*, Gary is the author of numerous books, including the award-winning bestsellers *The Grief Guidebook*, *Shattered: Surviving the Loss of a Child*, *Comfort for the Grieving Spouse's Heart*, and *Aftermath: Picking Up the Pieces After a Suicide*. Gary's books have won four international book awards and have been named finalists seven times. He has been featured on Dr. Laura, Belief Net, the Christian Broadcasting Network, Wellness, Thrive Global, and other major media and has well over 800 grief-related articles in print. Recipient of the Diane Duncam Award for Excellence in Hospice Care, Gary is a popular keynote, conference, and seminar speaker at a wide variety of venues.

Gary loves being a husband and father. He has seven adopted children. He enjoys hockey, corny jokes, good puns, and colorful Hawaiian shirts. Gary and his wife Jen and family live in Texas.

Visit Gary at www.garyroe.com.

Don't forget to download your free eBook (PDF):

Grief: 9 Things I Wish I Had Known

https://www.garyroe.com/grief-9-things-i-wish-i-had-known-ebook/

ACKNOWLEDGMENTS

Special thanks for my amazing wife Jen for her constant support and encouragement. Thank you for partnering with me in helping grieving hearts heal and grow.

Special thanks to Peggy Sanders and Kelli Levey Reynolds for their keen proofreading and editorial assistance. I appreciate you more than you know.

Thanks to Maria Wiggins of Hospice Brazos Valley for the title of this book. Your creativity and commitment to excellence are inspiring.

Thanks to my wonderful Advance Reader Team for their corrections, feedback, and input. You make every book much better.

Thanks to Glendon Haddix of Streetlight Graphics for his artistic skill and expertise in design and formatting. Your artistry continues to bring healing and hope to many.

AN URGENT PLEA
HELP OTHER GRIEVING HEARTS

Dear Reader,

Others are hurting and grieving today. You can help.

How?

With a simple, heartfelt review.

Could you take a few moments and write a 1-3 sentence review of *Grieving the Write Way Journal and Workbook* and leave it on the site you purchased the book from?

And if you want to help even more, you could leave the same review on the *Grieving the Write Way Journal and Workbook* book page on Goodreads.

Your review counts and will help reach others who could benefit from this book.

Thanks for considering this. I read these reviews as well, and your comments and feedback assist me in producing more quality resources for grieving hearts.

Thank you!

Warmly,

Gary

Don't forget to download your free eBook (PDF):
Grief: 9 Things I Wish I Had Known
https://www.garyroe.com/grief-9-things-i-wish-i-had-known-ebook/

www.ingramcontent.com/pod-product-compliance
Lightning Source LLC
Chambersburg PA
CBHW030148100526
44592CB00009B/171